To Paul —

Plug Uglies

A Scrapbook of Boston Organized Crime

HOWIE CARR

Frandel, LLC

Howie Carr

Cover photo: Some of the 1950s Brinks robbers, finally under arrest in 1956. In center, smoking, is Fat Tony Pino.

ISBN: 978-0-9860372-7-6 (paperback)
ISBN: 978-0-9860372-8-3 (epub)
ISBN: 978-0-9860372-9-0 (epdf)

Library of Congress Control Number: 2014948153

Printed in the United States of America.

Table of Contents

Acknowledgments

Once again, so many people contributed to the production of this book in such a short amount of time that I hope I don't miss thanking anyone who should be included in this brief list.

First of all, my wife Kathy, who handled all the production details—the partnership with Bookmasters, cover design, new magnets, the book-signing schedule, etc.

Two of my daughters—Carolyn and Tina—greatly helped their computer-challenged father, with varying amounts of snide remarks about my Stone Age ways. Also, thanks to Charlotte for coming with me to Boston to help take pictures.

Outside of the family, I certainly wish to thank my radio producer, Nancy "Sandy" Shack, who kept has kept track of an immense amount of crime-related material for a number of years. Also, thanks to Anthony Amore who quickly edited the book.

Thanks to everyone at the Boston *Herald*, starting with publisher Pat Purcell, editor Joe Sciacca and managing editor John Strahinich, for allowing me the use of *Herald* photographs. Also at the *Herald*, thanks to head photographers Jim Mahoney and Arthur Pollock, who tracked down my ancient mug shots, and head librarian Martha Reagan, who almost always found the obscure, 50-year-old clipping that I'd requested. Thanks also to *Herald* photographer Mark Garfinkel, who took many of the photos, especially during Whitey Bulger's 2013 trial. Darren Duarte of the Massachusetts Department of Correction patiently rounded up as many of the ancient DOC mugshots as he could find. I appreciate his efforts, and I hope the new governor does as well.

Thanks also to David Brow of the *Lowell Sun,* who shared his photo of the three convicted (and one unindicted coconspirator) speakers of the Massachusetts House of Representatives. Also, thanks to Gwen Gage at *The Boston Herald* for helping with the Boston show and Dan Busa of Busa Wines for a great show in Burlington.

Thanks too to all my radio affiliates that have supported my *Night of Crime* tours which served as a launching pad for both *Rifleman* and *Ratman.* Bob Adams at WGAN, Sean Davey at WHYN, Sheila and Bob Vinikoor at WNTK, Bruce Biette at WVOM, Kurt Carberry at WCRN, Bob Cox at WKBK and Allison Makkay Davis at WXTK—I trust we'll all continue to be together, well into the future.

At Bookmasters, I couldn't ask for a better project director than Jen Welsch. Her turnaround time is astonishing. Thanks also to Ken Fultz, David Hetherington, and everyone else in Ashland who helped out so much.

As always, many others contributed, but it would be doing them a disservice to name them. Those are my "sources." They provided me with most of these photos, especially the mugshots, which otherwise might never have been seen again. Some of the photos in this book were literally salvaged from trashcans in government buildings by people who knew a historical document when they saw one, or several.

And finally, thanks to you, the readers, who have supported these efforts.

I hope you enjoy reading *Plug Uglies* as much as I enjoyed putting it together.

Howie Carr

Introduction

This is a scrapbook, more or less. For more than 30 years, I've been covering Boston politics and organized crime—but I repeat myself. It has often been said that history repeats itself, but as Ira Gershwin might say, it ain't necessarily so.

Of course certain patterns do reoccur. For example, during Prohibition, South Boston's leading "sportsman" (as leading gangsters were invariably called, until well into the 1960s) was a Boston cop fired in the 1919 police strike named Dan Carroll. His brother was state Sen. Ed Carroll.

I called the book *Plug Uglies* because that's what these guys were, thugs or villains. The Plug Uglies were

Dan Carroll: a leading "sportsman." This was 40 years before the Bulgers, Whitey and Billy.

a 19th-century street gang that originated in Baltimore and quickly muscled its way into city politics.

They took part in the draft riots in New York City in 1863, according to one of the newspapers, because "the scoundrels cannot afford to miss this golden opportunity of indulging their brutal natures... and at the same time serving their colleagues, the Democrats."

So yes, these guys in Boston were definitely Plug Uglies.

I have also included some material on those Democrat politicians— the connections between the State House and City Hall and the guys on the corner were undeniable. Look at how many corrupt sheriffs Gov. Mike Dukakis appointed. All of his administrations were awash in corruption, and his final term, 1987-91, represented Whitey Bulger's apogee of power. This was the era when the mere questioning of Whitey at a Logan Airport security gate could lead to the instantaneous transfer of the state cop who had the audacity to question the Senate president's brother as he attempted to smuggle $100,000 cash out of the country to Canada.

One housing court judge had his budget gutted in 1988 after he refused to hire an unqualified crony of the Bulgers. Running for president, Dukakis didn't dare to restore the cut funds, leading the judge to utter the famous question: "How can Dukakis stand up to the Russians if he can't stand up to a corrupt midget?"

IN THIS wrap-up, I've tried to use as much material as possible that I never got around to using in the earlier books, or have come across since the end of Whitey Bulger's trial in 2013. I do a lot of book signings, and I run into people who have photographs or documents that haven't seen the light of day in 30 or 40 years, if ever.

They come from relatives of the plug uglies themselves, or cops, or lawyers, or even, in some cases, the hoodlums themselves. One day in 2011 a woman wanted to know if she could trade me a photograph of an 11-year-old Whitey and his "gang" in return for a copy of my latest book, *Hitman*.

What a steal! A couple of days later we ran the photo in the *Herald*, blown up to a half page. Somebody wrote a snide blog a couple of days later in the *Globe* chuckling over both papers' archaeological-like obsession

Early photo of Whitey Bulger, second from left, circa 1940

with new Whitey material. This was in June 2011. A couple of days later, Whitey was captured in Santa Monica, and I was on the phone with *ABC World News Tonight*, listening to their pleas for the Whitey-as-Bowery-Boy photo.

Boston organized crime will never be what it was in the 20th century. Racing is dead and the State Lottery Commission has an iron lock on the numbers racket. As for the "morals" crimes, you may not believe what you read in the chapter entitled "The Departed."

Any number of hoodlums were charged with "lewd and lascivious cohabitation," otherwise known as shacking up. Sammy Lindenbaum was repeatedly lugged for performing abortions; today he might be holding press conferences with leading Democrat politicians about the need for "buffer zones" around "women's health clinics." The one black gangland victim in "The Departed" actually took a pinch in 1958 for, of all things, "fornication."

Another popular roust back then was for a crime that has taken on a whole new meaning in this era of transgendered rights—"being abroad in the night." That's one word, by the way, "abroad."

Going through a batch of ancient mugshots, I came upon a guy named Rocky Palladino. Simply by virtue of his fine fedora he made the cut, but I wanted to know more about him.

It turns out he owned a string of thoroughbred horses, including one, Little Beans, that ran in the 1941 Kentucky Derby. Much to Rocky's chagrin, the loudmouth LA mobster Mickey Cohen once casually dropped his name as one of the leading layoff men in the country, which according to Rocky did not enhance his social standing in blueblood Boston.

The most fascinating fact about Rocky, though, was his command performance before a Suffolk County grand jury in 1954, when he was asked, according to the *Traveler,* about "the appearance of Christine Jorgenson at his night club."

Christine Jorgenson—the most famous transsexual of the 1950's. And

Rocky Palladino: another
local sportsman

it was apparently borderline banned-in-Boston to have such a person in your licensed establishment. Liquor licenses had been lost for lesser morals violations.

District Attorney Garrett Byrne, who as recently as 1978 was making busts of gay bars a staple of his reelection campaigns, told reporters Palladino was questioned about Jorgenson's "doubtful sex."

"It is a disgrace that the decent people of Boston should be visited with the appearance of such an 'entertainer,'" Byrne harrumphed. "I know nothing that will do more to increase juvenile delinquency than appearances of entertainers of this sort."

This was 60 years ago. Even as recently as the 1988 presidential election, it was a scandal that Gov. Dukakis' state government had paid for one—one!—sex-change operation, although of course it added to the embarrassment that the Medicaid recipient was a New Hampshire resident, and that the Commonwealth also paid for his/her post-operative hormone therapy in Montreal.

Now, however, sex changes are routinely covered under the state's MassHealth program. Why should welfare recipients be denied the right to "reassign" their gender any more than a homeless female junkie should be turned down for the fertility drugs that will enhance the chances of giving birth to multiple drug-addicted infants who will immediately be added to the state's burgeoning welfare rolls?

Eddie Connors: wrong number

POOR PEOPLE really were desperate in the days covered by this book. Until 1968, any welfare in Massachusetts came from the cities and towns— and when your neighbors knew that they were supporting you out of their property taxes, they tended to be a lot stingier.

Gangsters, of course, were not exactly at the top of the list when it came to thinking about charity beginning at home. Whitey Bulger's brother, Billy, wrote in his memoir, *While the Music Lasts,* how as a young lawyer he defended a Boston veterans agent named Birmingham who had improperly arranged for the family of imprisoned gangster Alan "Suitcase" Fidler to get on the city dole.

Fidler was the underworld partner of Eddie Connors, murdered by Billy's brother Whitey in 1976. As for the veterans' agent, Birmingham was himself the brother of a gangster, Thomas Birmingham, who was shot to death in a Charlestown rooming house in 1969. His nephew and namesake later went on to succeed Billy Bulger as president of the state Senate.

Suitcase Fidler

Birmingham's first election had been arranged by Bulger; they had so much in common that the older Bulger seemed to be the younger man's mentor.

Boston truly was a small town in those days.

IN THOSE days, newspapers still ruled the media roost. There was the *Globe* and the *Evening Globe,* the morning *Herald* and the afternoon *Traveler,* and the Hearst-owned *Record* and the afternoon *American,* which merged in 1961 to make the *Record American,* which published around the clock "Yesterday's News Tomorrow" as the joke went. The *Record* was the paper sold in the barrooms, where a numbers player could learn if he had won that day's "nigger pool" number.

The *Christian Science Monitor* was also a legitimate daily of sorts, and the Boston *Post,* once the largest-circulation newspaper in the United States, had only gone out of business a few years earlier, in 1956. The old Yankee newspaper, the *Evening Transcript,* where Henry Cabot Lodge had cut his teeth as a cub reporter, folded in 1939.

With all newspapers in essence publishing around the clock, competition was fierce, and the two biggest crime stories of the early 1960's were the Boston Strangler and the so-called Irish gang war and all the assorted mayhem it brought along in its wake.

In those days newspaper reporters consisted of two distinct groups— the first of which were the legmen, the guys out on the street, almost always city guys themselves, who'd graduated straight from high school or the military into newspaper internships, skipping the soon-to-be-obligatory four years of college. The legmen had often known the local cops and the gangsters their entire lives; sometimes they were related. The other reporters were known as "rewritemen," or "college boys," as they were sometimes derisively called.

The rewritemen stayed back in the city room, took dictation from the legmen, and cobbled together their stories, which were often phoned in from the nearest bar where a legman could get a "dimey" or a "musty"— a 10-cent draft, half dark Pickwick Ale and half Narranganett lager beer. ("Hi Neighbor, Have a 'Gansett!") At the end of their shifts, down at the Blue Sands, the Hearst legmen might spring for a shot or two of Green River whisky, which they'd pour into their musties. That way, if their wives insisted on smelling their breaths, as they usually did, the booze smell would be overpowered by the hops.

One of the top rewritemen at the *Record* was Harold Banks, who'd graduated in the same class at Boston Latin with Theodore White, the famous Time Inc. journalist who wrote the best-selling *Making of the President* book series. Later Banks haggled with Joe Barboza over ghostwriting his autobiography.

Visitors to Boston often commented on the appalling quality of the local dailies. As far as Hub sheets were concerned, the world was composed of only two classes of women. Some had dark hair:

Others were, well, not brunette:

But they all led lives straight out of the B movies of the day:

The newspapers couldn't get enough of underworld murders. Mystery molls were a staple of the genre, often delivered to posh love nests by "mystery cabbies." Any pre-rubout visit to a restaurant would inevitably lead to police dragnets for a "mystery waiter." These were the days when the papers, the tabloids especially, could keep a juicy story pumped up for weeks. In New York, the legendary actor John Garfield suffered a fatal heart attack while in the saddle, so to speak, with a society dame. The tabloids went wild.

The New York dailies kept the Garfield story going for 16 days, but finally, even the most imaginative headline writers were running out of steam. At a budget meeting for the next edition, everyone sat glumly around the table, trying to come up with something to keep the story going one day longer.

Finally, an editor piped up.

"I've got it," he said. "Here's the headline: 'John Garfield Still Dead!'"

IN BOSTON the Balliros were a well-known family of ne'er-do-wells, with

Rocco Balliro: thug in love

a few lawyers thrown in for good measure. Rocco Balliro fell hard for a moll named Toby Zimmerman Wagner, a 21-year-old mother whose husband was doing a bit in state prison. One crime led to another, and in January 1963 Rocco and Toby and the infant were on the run, holed up and surrounded by the police.

Hundreds of rounds later, when the shootout was over, Toby and her son were dead, and Rocco had escaped. This story was so big even the Boston Strangler got bumped off the front page for a few days.

Finally, Toby was buried, along with her son. Rocco remained on the lam. The story, it seemed, had finally run its course. But then one of the city's

Toby Zimmerman Wagner:
the wages of sin

more resourceful legmen got an idea. This was a guy prepared for any eventuality. In the trunk of his car he carried a bra, to be discarded at the scene of a rape ("Cops Find Mystery Bra"). He also had throw-down knives. In his glove compartment he carried matchboxes from some of the city's more infamous gay bars, in case he decided to redirect a confirmed-bachelor murder story in the direction of a mystery pal.

First the legman found a floral shop a couple of towns away from where Toby had been buried. He bought a large bouquet with cash, taking care to make sure it could not be traced back. Then he called his city desk to breathlessly dictate the big news to one of the college boys—a witness had just called the local police department in the town where Toby was buried to report that he had just seen someone who looked exactly like Rocco Balliro dropping a bouquet of flowers on his lover's grave.

He called the paper before the cops because it would take at least an hour or so to get an extra edition onto the streets, and the legman wanted to make sure his paper had an insurmountable head start on the competition.

As the front-page replate was being set in print back in Winthrop Square, the legman drove to the cemetery, hurriedly tossed the bouquet onto the fresh grave, and then drove to a previously-scouted, out-of-the-way pay phone, where he called the police to alert them to Rocco's alleged appearance before quickly hanging up.

The other legmen quickly figured out that the story's timeline was too good to be true, but nobody ratted him out. He had beaten them, after all, fair and square.

THIS WAS the environment the Bulgers grew up in. As a young state rep, Billy Bulger sometimes played cards with the Hearst legmen—their game was hearts. Whitey would, and did, think nothing of threatening newspapermen—most of them came out of the same socioeconomic class as he and his family. Of course, just as Whitey was leery of shaking down "legitimate" businessmen, he likewise seldom threatened anyone in the press unless they were either Irish or Italian—from "the neighborhood," so to speak. The *Globe* newsroom was increasingly populated by trust-funded Ivy Leaguers, children of privilege who might not understand that the rules of the city game required keeping one's mouth shut, no matter what. Whitey gave the "college boys" of Morrissey Boulevard a good leaving-alone, to quote Eddie Coyle.

The first reporter he seriously shook down was Paul Corsetti, a Vietnam vet and a second-generation Hearst legman. His father Eddie had been the overnight police reporter for the *American*. One of his nightly duties was to deliver a gallon of elderberry wine and two packs of Spud cigarettes to the home of Walter Howey, the Hearst editor upon whom the crusty Walter Burns character in the play and movie *The Front Page* had been based. Before his death in 1954, Howey almost went to prison for stabbing a young man in the elevator of his Beacon Hill townhouse who had somehow managed to look at him the wrong way.

In 1980, Whitey murdered Louie Litif, another of Zip Connolly's FBI

James Matera: murdered by Louis Litif

snitches. Litif had executed another Southie hood, James Matera, without Whitey's okay. This was a capital offense. Litif was shot at Triple O's and his body ended up in his wife's car, abandoned outside Larry Baione's laundromat in the South End.

Corsetti sensed a good story, and began making inquiries. One evening he got a call from an anonymous caller offering enough tantalizing details to get Corsetti to agree to meet him at a barroom in Quincy Market.

Corsetti had recently spent a few days in jail for refusing to reveal a source, so he was fairly recognizable at

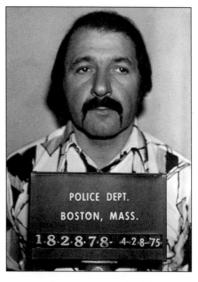

Louis Litif: murdered by Whitey Bulger

the time. As Corsetti waited for his source to show up, a trim middle-aged guy grabbed the stool next to him and asked him if he were Paul Corsetti. After a couple of minutes of conversation, Corsetti politely said he was waiting for someone.

"You're waiting for me, motherfucker," Whitey Bulger snarled. Then he took a slip of paper out of his breast pocket and read off the license plates and models of the Corsetti family's cars, their address in suburban Medford, and most ominously, the address of the day-care center where they dropped off their young daughter each morning.

The next morning Corsetti showed up in the city room wearing a holster with a .38 revolver. He went to police headquarters on Berkeley Street and was told that the cops "had" Whitey for approximately 40 hits. Eventually Whitey was calmed down; apparently he'd somehow convinced himself that Corsetti was going after his brother, not him.

But the word was now out there, and nobody wanted to tangle with Whitey. Even the clueless Ivy Leaguers at the *Globe* realized that inheriting $20 million, or a mansion on Nantucket or in the Hamptons, didn't mean much if you were dead.

The *Globe* not only stopped reporting on Whitey; they decided to make him into a folk hero, the man who "kept the drugs out of Southie." When one of their photographers got pictures of a City of Boston work crew installing curbs in the parking lot of Whitey's newly-extorted liquor store, the editors refused to print them as the photographer later testified under oath in federal court. Like the editors in the old John Ford movie, they'd decided that when the legend becomes fact, print the legend.

I STARTED writing again about Whitey around 1985, when the trial of Mafia underboss Jerry Angiulo and his brothers began in federal court. Whitey's name was mentioned on an almost-daily basis, so I thought I was safe. My main problem, I believe, was the same as Paul Corsetti's—Whitey thought I was going after his brother Billy. And in my case anyway, he was right.

But what is a reporter supposed to do when he has videotape of the former mayor of Boston, Kevin White, explaining to Channel 2's Chris Lydon the real source of the power behind the man who would soon be known as "the Corrupt Midget":

"If my brother threatened to kill you, you'd be nothing but nice to me."

After printing that story, I heard from a couple of reporters who were tight with corrupt FBI agent Zip Connolly. They said I should watch myself in Southie. No problem—I always did. The bigger headache I had was my second job at Channel 56 on Morrissey Boulevard next to the *Globe.* To get there from the *Herald,* I had to drive past the South Boston Liquor Mart.

In the warm weather, Whitey would hold court on the sidewalk in the rotary outside the liquor store, wearing dark glasses, waving to his friends as if he were a candidate doing an election-eve standout during rush hour. Think Johnny Depp in *Black Mass*—they got Whitey's mid-1980's look exactly right.

It was disconcerting, to say the least, to see a serial killer operating so brazenly, with total protection from the law. What was almost as outrageous was how, during every election, the political candidates from Southie would vie to have their signs in the front window of his packy. They wanted that seal of approval, the imprimatur, from the Town's leading mass murderer and cocaine dealer.

Working two jobs, some nights I had worked up quite a thirst by the time I left the TV station. But if I didn't plan on hoisting a few at J.J. Foley's, I never stopped by the South Boston Liquor Mart. I always cut across to Andrew Square to grab a couple of beers for the ride home.

The anchor at Ch. 56 was Jack Hynes, the son of the mayor who'd finally ended the political career of James Michael Curley back in 1949. Jack lived in Southie at the time, and one night he stopped by Stippo's old place to pick up a bottle of wine.

You can read what happened next in the State Police affidavit below:

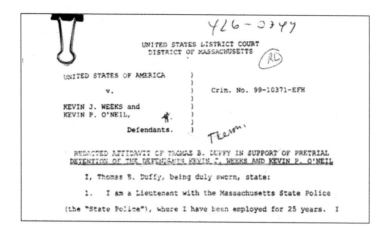

After Jack told me that story the next day, I decided maybe I'd been taking the whole situation too lightly. I started driving home a different way every night. I stopped arranging meetings with anyone I didn't know. One thing I didn't do was call the cops. Oh sure, I knew most cops were all right, but if I'd called, word would have gotten back to Whitey. It would have been like showing fear to a dog.

Besides, seriously, what could the cops do for me or anybody else in such a situation? I knew that the Bulgers kept the local FBI on a short leash. Whitey paid them directly. And if the G-men played ball, when they retired there would likely be a six-figure, no-heavy-lifting job waiting for them at one of the utilities that just happened to be regulated by Billy Bulger's state government. Conversely, if they went after Whitey, well, they weren't going to get him anyway, so what was the point of cutting off your nose to spite your face?

The Boston cops were okay, most of them—after all, Mayor Ray Flynn had turned Billy Bulger down cold when he wanted to have Zip Connolly appointed as Boston police commissioner in 1984. A made member of an organized-crime family as police commissioner—Al Capone himself had never dreamed of accomplishing such a feat. But Raybo had even appointed Mickey Roache, the brother of the Mullen gang member whom Whitey had paralyzed for life in a barroom shooting in 1971.

Then there were the state cops. The MSP were the most vulnerable of them all. As president of the state Senate, Billy Bulger controlled their budget directly, and he had no qualms about throwing his weight around. The only pol at the State House who ever dared to stand

Bobby Ford: Buddy Roache was shot in his West Broadway bar.

up to Billy's machinations on behalf of his brother was one-term Gov. Ed King.

Yet the *Globe,* which trembled in abject fear of the Bulgers in their heyday, excoriated both King and Flynn. It didn't matter that they were Democrats, at least nominally. What made them so unacceptable to the Beautiful People was the fact that they were anti-abortion Irish Catholics from the city. Somehow, though, despite their lack of Ivy League credentials, King and Flynn were able to see through the Bulger "mystique" much more clearly than *Globe* bluebloods who found the little man's faux erudition and Irish brogue so amusing.

BILLY BULGER thrived in an atmosphere of intimidation and terror. It is said that in the kingdom of the blind, the one-eyed man shall lead. Billy at least knew who, and what, he was. He was operating under no illusions. Most of the other pols at the State House were legends in their own mind. They didn't believe in papal infallibility, but their own… that was another matter altogether.

Just to cite one example, here's a letter from the ever-sanctimonious Michael S. Dukakis, brushing off yet another plea for mercy from Louie Greco, who at this point had already

Louie Greco: a World War II hero

spent 18 years in prison after being framed by the FBI for a murder he did not commit. Dukakis assigned the review of the Greco case to one of his incompetent affirmative-action hires, future federal felon Dianne Wilkerson.

Imagine—your fate decided by a corrupt woman who would soon be a state senator, and who would herself end up in prison, convicted of stuffing a $1,000 bribe in her bra.

The question isn't how Whitey Bulger lasted so long. The question is, in an environment as corrupt as Beacon Hill, how was he ever captured at all?

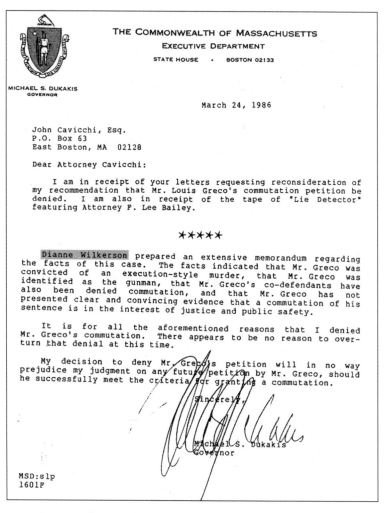

THE COMMONWEALTH OF MASSACHUSETTS

EXECUTIVE DEPARTMENT

STATE HOUSE · BOSTON 02133

MICHAEL S. DUKAKIS
GOVERNOR

March 24, 1986

John Cavicchi, Esq.
P.O. Box 63
East Boston, MA 02128

Dear Attorney Cavicchi:

I am in receipt of your letters requesting reconsideration of my recommendation that Mr. Louis Greco's commutation petition be denied. I am also in receipt of the tape of "Lie Detector" featuring Attorney F. Lee Bailey.

✶✶✶✶✶

Dianne Wilkerson prepared an extensive memorandum regarding the facts of this case. The facts indicated that Mr. Greco was convicted of an execution-style murder, that Mr. Greco was identified as the gunman, that Mr. Greco's co-defendants have also been denied commutation, and that Mr. Greco has not presented clear and convincing evidence that a commutation of his sentence is in the interest of justice and public safety.

It is for all the aforementioned reasons that I denied Mr. Greco's commutation. There appears to be no reason to over-turn that denial at this time.

My decision to deny Mr. Greco's petition will in no way prejudice my judgment on any future petition by Mr. Greco, should he successfully meet the criteria for granting a commutation.

Sincerely,

Michael S. Dukakis
Governor

MSD:slp
1601F

Dianne Wilkerson: thumbs down to the plea of an innocent man

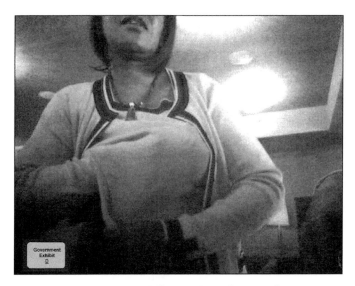

Senator Dianne Wilkerson, D–Roxbury: Smile,
you're on Candid Camera!

I MOVED out of Somerville and ended up in the same suburban town as Kevin Weeks' brother. I lived across the street from a graveyard, a fact that appeared to delight the Bulgers to no end. Soon they were talking not only about how they'd tried to intimidate me in the old days, but what they were planning to do to me now that we'd all moved out to the suburbs.

Again, quoting from the 1999 State Police report on Weeks:

> 81. WEEKS also has threatened, in a veiled fashion, a member of the local news media in an apparent effort to chill that reporter, who has regularly described WEEKS in print as a member of Bulger's and Flemmi's criminal organization, from writing about WEEKS. In approximately February of 1996 or 1997, a photographer from the Boston Herald went to a local tanning salon to photograph persons tanning themselves during the winter months. WEEKS and his girlfriend were at the tanning salon. The photographer attempted to photograph WEEKS' girlfriend. WEEKS rebuked him and then engaged him in a discussion regarding Herald columnist Howie Carr, the reporter referred to above. WEEKS told the photographer, in substance, "We used to know where Howie lived; it's across from a graveyard." The photographer relayed this statement to Carr, who lived at one time across from a cemetery. In addition, in approximately 1987 or 1988, a

It seems unlikely that Weeks ever really had me in his sights. At Whitey's trial in 2013, he couldn't remember my address. More tellingly, earlier on *60 Minutes*, he had recalled lying on the edge of the cemetery, rifle in hand, drawing a bead on me. The problem with his story is that a stone wall, maybe four or five feet tall, separates the graveyard from the street.

If Weeks were lying in the weeds, he would have needed a Rube Goldberg-esque rifle, one in which the bullet went straight, then stopped, after which it began traveling up through the barrel for about 18 inches, then stopped again before once more changing direction and flying straight out of the barrel.

In short, Weeks' tall tale puts the magic back in the magic bullet theory.

Still, I remember how happy I was that morning in early 1995 when I heard on the radio that Whitey had taken it on the lam. The usual suspects were spewing out their usual crap—the end of an era, "our" gangster, Jimmy Cagney, etc.

But it took another 16-plus years to catch Whitey. The FBI just wasn't up to the task. Not only were the G-men feuding with other law-enforcement agencies, they were also battling among themselves.

For instance, in 2000 the LA office sent out this press release:

U.S. Department of Justice

Federal Bureau of Investigation

In Reply, Please Refer to
File No.

PRESS RELEASE

One of the FBI's most wanted Top Ten Fugitives JAMES J. (Whitey) BULGER may currently be located in Orange County. Recent information developed by the television show "America's Most Wanted" has resulted in sightings of BULGER and his companion CATHERINE E. GREIG in southern California.

BULGER, a major Organized Crime figure in Boston, Massachusetts, was indicted in January 1995 with a New England Crime Family Boss and five others. BULGER controlled a criminal organization in Boston that was closely associated with La Cosa Nostra. He is being sought for extortion and federal racketeering charges. BULGER is also suspected in approximately 20 unsolved homicides. He has been a fugitive since the arrest warrants were issued. A $250,000.00 reward is being offered for information leading to the arrest of BULGER.

BULGER is believed to be traveling by motor vehicle with CATHERINE E. GREIG, his long time girl friend. GREIG was charged with harboring a federal fugitive in April 1997, and is also a fugitive.

On January 29, 2000 BULGER and GREIG were profiled on America's Most Wanted, and based on that show a positive sighting of GREIG was made in Orange County. GREIG is known to frequent beauty salons to have her hair dyed. She only visits a salon once to have her hair done and usually brings her own hair dye with her. While in the salon, a male whom she identifies as her husband, waits in the car for her.

Any information regarding BULGER or GREIG should be immediately provided to the FBI at 714)542-8825 in Santa Ana, or (310)477-6565 in Los Angeles for 24 hour response.

A couple of hours later, the Boston office responded with a press release of its own:

U.S. Department of Justice

Federal Bureau of Investigation

In Reply, Please Refer to
File No.

Suite 600
One Center Plaza
Boston, MA 02108-1801
April 5, 2000

PRESS RELEASE

Recently, the Top Ten Fugitive, James J. "Whitey" Bulger was featured on the television show "America's Most Wanted". As a result of that broadcast, information was received regarding a possible sighting of Catherine E. Greig in Orange County, California. Greig is believed to be traveling with Bulger.

Based upon investigation by the FBI's Los Angeles Field Office, it has been determined that an individual resembling Catherine E. Greig was observed at a beauty salon in Southern California. There was no confirmed sighting of Bulger. All necessary investigation has been conducted and there is no additional information as to the whereabouts of Bulger and Greig.

The fugitive investigation of Bulger continues to be aggressively pursued by the Boston FBI Office.

Considering that Whitey was captured in Santa Monica—11 years later—which FBI office do you suppose was more interested in capturing the fugitive?

LIKE THE poor, the criminals will always be with us. But the days of gangsters wielding the kind of life-and-death power Whitey Bulger once exercised appear over.

Whitey was a multi-millionaire, with clout at the highest levels of state government and law enforcement. Consider the pudgy plug ugly whom some believe is the current boss of the Boston Mafia, one Carmen "the

Cheeseman" DiNunzio. He is 56 years old, and is currently imprisoned at the federal penitentiary in Loretto PA.

Here is a description of DiNunzio from 2012:

"He has been diagnosed with diabetes, high blood pressure, asthma, fluid around his heart, high cholesterol and back problems. He is prescribed insulin, medication for high blood pressure and cholesterol, and fluid tablets. . .DiNunzio has been collecting disability income for the last 15 years. . .He has minimal financial resources. He indicated that he receives a disability payment of $800 per month and that he owns a 1998 Audi automobile. . .He does not own any real estate."

Carmen DiNunzio: the Cheeseman

In his battle with the FBI, even at 450 pounds, DiNunzio was fighting above his weight class. For example, one of the Cheeseman's favorite restaurants in Chinatown was Billy Tse's. As DiNunzio later discovered, the feds had bugged every single table in the restaurant, so that no matter where he sat, the Cheeseman would be recorded.

It hardly seems sporting to wire every table. When former Mafia boss Cadillac Frank Salemme was doing business out of the Busy Bee in Brookline, in order to be recorded he had to sit at the one table with the wired napkin dispenser.

Whitey was a serial killer; the Cheeseman had an eating disorder. One day, meeting with a made member of the Gambino Crime family at My Cousin Vinny's restaurant in Malden, DiNunzio recalled a North End meeting with one of his Rhode Island collectors after which they were both rousted by the feds, who took $5,000 in cash from "the boss."

After the feds left him, broke and dejected on Endicott Street, DiNunzio recalled his first reaction. He said he told his guy:

"Come on, let's go have a steak for lunch because we are probably going to get pinched tomorrow."

They're just not making plug uglies like Whitey Bulger anymore.

The Departed

What follows is the Mass. State Police's "Blue Bulletin," so called because it was originally printed on light blue paper. It records the murders and careers of 32 gangland victims who died between 1963 and 1966. This copy was given to me by the wife of an old-time criminal lawyer who no longer had any use for either the "Blue Bulletin" or the documents I have used for the later chapters on the Great Plymouth Mail Truck Robbery and the messages from the Commissioner.

Be sure to check out the message at the beginning of the Blue Bulletin from the commissioner. L.L. Laughlin veers dangerously close to what might today be considered "hate speech" in Massachusetts:

"The organized police departments and *all* of their members are now being *challenged* by a handful of hoodlums in open defiance of the law and rights of the people who pay the bills."

The people who pay the bills? Since when do they count for anything in modern-day Massachusetts? Nowadays they're called "bitter clingers."

Whenever possible, the name of the actual murderer is included at the bottom of the page. Some crimes are still unsolved, at least officially. In two cases—John O'Neil and Anthony Sacramone—photos that were apparently not available to the police at the time have been added.

One of the more interesting cases is that of Francis Benjamin. His cause of death in 1964 is listed as "decapitation." Indeed, the ex-con was found headless, in the trunk of a car in South Boston. But his head was not chopped off until after his murder.

He was drinking at Stevie Flemmi's Roxbury lounge with Stevie, his brother Jimmy "the Bear" Flemmi, and the Flemmis' boss, Wimpy Bennett. Stevie alone survives among those who were there that night, and he doesn't seem to have ever indicated who pulled the trigger, or why exactly.

After the murder, the three killers apparently realized that they had used a gun left behind at the bar by one of their crooked cop friends. The hoods

John O'Neil

weren't sure of the gun's provenance, so they couldn't afford to have honest law-enforcement running ballistics tests on the bullets in Benjamin's head.

So they chopped off his head and well, you can read about the rest of it on his Blue Bulletin sheet.

The Benjamin story also has a postscript. In 1973, Francis R. Benjamin, Jr., age 19, was arrested and charged with the sniper slaying of a black youth in the D Street housing projects during the run-up to school busing in Boston. Benjamin's lawyer told the jury of the elder Benjamin's grisly slaying, pleading with them, "Don't send this kid to be murdered. Don't send him to the jungles of Walpole to be murdered as his father was." Benjamin was

Anthony Sacramone

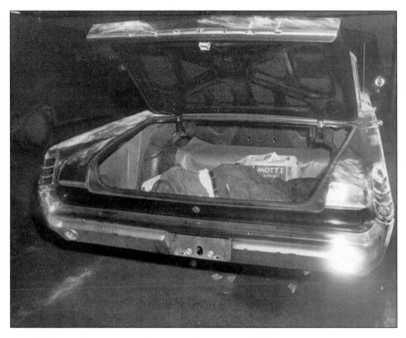

Missing: one head

Jimmy Flemmi and Frankie Benjamin. Killer and victim, in MCI-Norfolk

convicted of manslaughter, but in 1975 the verdict was overturned and he was acquitted at retrial.

Another murder with a backstory involved the late Paul Colicci, whose body was found smelling up in the trunk of a car in a Quincy motel parking lot on a hot summer day in July 1964.

Ex-con Colicci was running a scam at the time, selling "air coolers" door-to-door as air conditioners. He was partnered up with another Rhode Island guy who happened to be in the wrong place at the wrong time. But the Mafia wasn't interested in Colicci's latest two-bit grift. He had a price on his head because he had once written a letter to Raymond L.S. Patriarca, "the Man."

Colicci, a Rhode Island native, was doing a stretch for jewel robbery at the old Charlestown state prison in 1957 when he penned a note to "the Man." Prison authorities confiscated the letter, and it was read aloud to a U.S. Senate subcommittee a year before Colicci's murder.

"Hello, Boss," it began. "Do you notice how I respect you and call you boss? But do you have to leave me in jail? I wrote to you and Henry (Tameleo), but I didn't get an answer. . . Dear boss, get me a new lawyer and a new trial. Because I would like to be on the street. . . Please don't tell me you people are broke, because I know better.

"The Man"—Raymond Patriarca

Future state auditor Joe DeNucci poses with future
gangland-slaying victim Rico Sacramone.

Then came the clinching paragraph:

"I'm reading a novel, *Oliver Twist,* and it's all about a man named Fagan. He was a man who sent kids out to steal and then he would steal from them... Bye, Big boss. Paul."

You have to feel sorry for the widow of Leo "Iggy" Lowry, shot to death in September 1964. Her maiden name was Kathleen Murray, and her brother, John Murray, would be murdered in January 1965.

Some victims had strange occupations. Sammy Lindenbaum, age 67 when he was murdered in 1966, was described as a "paper boy." Raymond DiStasio was a "novelty stand operator" and Bobby Palladino a "fruit peddler."

Punchy McLaughlin, a "union delegate," had a tattoo of a "profile of a woman smoking cigarette."

As for John Barbieri, he had a couple of nicknames you don't hear much anymore: "Heeb" and "Jew." No one, though, had the moniker pinned on Philadelphia mobster Harry Stromberg—"Nig," as in "Nig Rosen."

On the page for slain Newton gangster Rocco DiSeglio, you may recognize the name of his associate—Joseph DeNucci. That was his fellow boxer, who would eventually become the longest-serving elected state auditor in the history of Massachusetts, from 1987 to 2011.

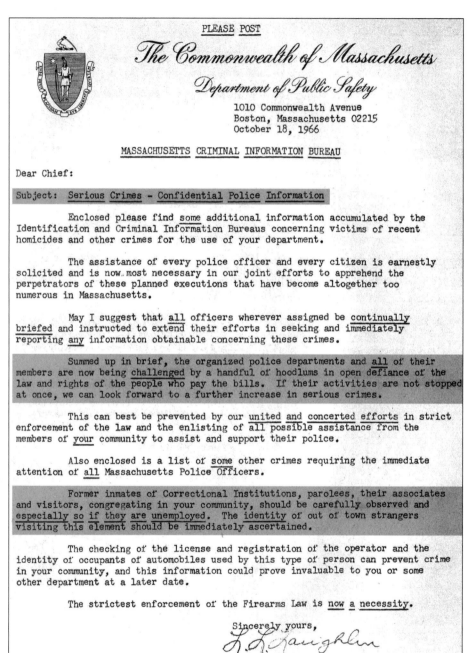

PLEASE POST

The Commonwealth of Massachusetts
Department of Public Safety

1010 Commonwealth Avenue
Boston, Massachusetts 02215
October 18, 1966

MASSACHUSETTS CRIMINAL INFORMATION BUREAU

Dear Chief:

Subject: Serious Crimes - Confidential Police Information

Enclosed please find some additional information accumulated by the Identification and Criminal Information Bureaus concerning victims of recent homicides and other crimes for the use of your department.

The assistance of every police officer and every citizen is earnestly solicited and is now most necessary in our joint efforts to apprehend the perpetrators of these planned executions that have become altogether too numerous in Massachusetts.

May I suggest that all officers wherever assigned be continually briefed and instructed to extend their efforts in seeking and immediately reporting any information obtainable concerning these crimes.

Summed up in brief, the organized police departments and all of their members are now being challenged by a handful of hoodlums in open defiance of the law and rights of the people who pay the bills. If their activities are not stopped at once, we can look forward to a further increase in serious crimes.

This can best be prevented by our united and concerted efforts in strict enforcement of the law and the enlisting of all possible assistance from the members of your community to assist and support their police.

Also enclosed is a list of some other crimes requiring the immediate attention of all Massachusetts Police Officers.

Former inmates of Correctional Institutions, parolees, their associates and visitors, congregating in your community, should be carefully observed and especially so if they are unemployed. The identity of out of town strangers visiting this element should be immediately ascertained.

The checking of the license and registration of the operator and the identity of occupants of automobiles used by this type of person can prevent crime in your community, and this information could prove invaluable to you or some other department at a later date.

The strictest enforcement of the Firearms Law is now a necessity.

Sincerely yours,

L. L. Laughlin
Commissioner of Public Safety

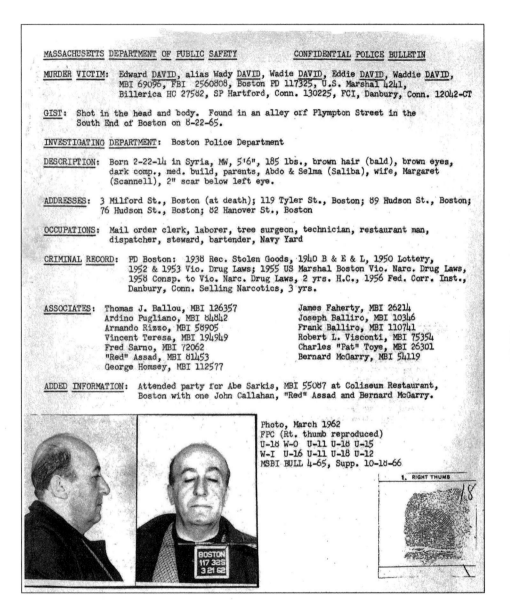

MASSACHUSETTS DEPARTMENT OF PUBLIC SAFETY   CONFIDENTIAL POLICE BULLETIN

MURDER VICTIM: Edward DAVID, alias Wady DAVID, Wadie DAVID, Eddie DAVID, Waddie DAVID,
                MBI 69096, FBI 2560808, Boston PD 117325, U.S. Marshal 4241,
                Billerica HC 27582, SP Hartford, Conn. 130225, FCI, Danbury, Conn. 12042-CT

GIST: Shot in the head and body. Found in an alley orf Plympton Street in the
       South End of Boston on 8-22-65.

INVESTIGATING DEPARTMENT: Boston Police Department

DESCRIPTION: Born 2-22-14 in Syria, MW, 5'6", 185 lbs., brown hair (bald), brown eyes,
              dark comp., med. build, parents, Abdo & Selma (Saliba), wife, Margaret
              (Scannell), 2" scar below left eye.

ADDRESSES: 3 Milford St., Boston (at death); 119 Tyler St., Boston; 89 Hudson St., Boston;
            76 Hudson St., Boston; 82 Hanover St., Boston

OCCUPATIONS: Mail order clerk, laborer, tree surgeon, technician, restaurant man,
              dispatcher, steward, bartender, Navy Yard

CRIMINAL RECORD: PD Boston: 1938 Rec. Stolen Goods, 1940 B & E & L, 1950 Lottery,
                  1952 & 1953 Vio. Drug Laws; 1955 US Marshal Boston Vio. Narc. Drug Laws,
                  1958 Consp. to Vio. Narc. Drug Laws, 2 yrs. H.C., 1956 Fed. Corr. Inst.,
                  Danbury, Conn. Selling Narcotics, 3 yrs.

ASSOCIATES: Thomas J. Ballou, MBI 126357   James Faherty, MBI 26214
             Ardino Pugliano, MBI 84842   Joseph Balliro, MBI 10346
             Armando Rizzo, MBI 58905   Frank Balliro, MBI 110741
             Vincent Teresa, MBI 194949   Robert L. Visconti, MBI 75354
             Fred Sarno, MBI 72062   Charles "Pat" Toye, MBI 26301
             "Red" Assad, MBI 81453   Bernard McGarry, MBI 54119
             George Homsey, MBI 112577

ADDED INFORMATION: Attended party for Abe Sarkis, MBI 55087 at Coliseum Restaurant,
                    Boston with one John Callahan, "Red" Assad and Bernard McGarry.

Photo, March 1962
FPC (Rt. thumb reproduced)
U-18 W-O U-11 U-18 U-15
W-I U-16 U-11 U-18 U-12
MSBI BULL 4-65, Supp. 10-18-66

1. RIGHT THUMB

BOSTON
117 325
3 21 62

Murder unsolved

MASSACHUSETTS DEPARTMENT OF PUBLIC SAFETY   CONFIDENTIAL POLICE BULLETIN

MURDER VICTIM: David M. SIDLAUSKAS, alias David Martin SIDLAUSKAS, MBI 272147,
FBI 582541E, PD Boston 122583

GIST: Shot through left chest and right elbow in pump house on Moon Island Road,
Squantum, near the bridge leading to the Long Island Hospital on 4-24-66.
Subject apparently staggered out of pump house and collapsed on the road.
Body found by two hospital nurses on their way to work about 6:30 A.M.

INVESTIGATING DEPARTMENTS: Quincy PD and Mass. State Police

DESCRIPTION: Born 2-2-44 in Boston, MW, 5'11", 150 lbs., brown hair, blue eyes,
med. build, med. comp., parents, Casey & Ann (Allen), wife, Rita

ADDRESSES: 8 Norwell St., Dorchester   33 Mt. Vernon St., Dorchester
12 Tuckerman St., South Boston   569 E 7th St., South Boston

OCCUPATIONS: Machine operator, laborer

CRIMINAL RECORD: 1962 Norfolk Co. HC Falsely Alt. MV Cert. of Reg. 1 mo.,
1963 PD Boston SP Larc MV, 5 yrs. 1 day Susp., 1965 Open & Gross Lewd.

ASSOCIATES: Ronald Jackman, MBI 601250   Anthony Veranis, MBI 178926 (victim)

ADDED INFORMATION: Victim and Veranis seen together in Dorchester Cafe on Saturday
before the murder. One Ronald Jackman, MBI 601250, was arrested,
tried, and acquitted of murder in this case.

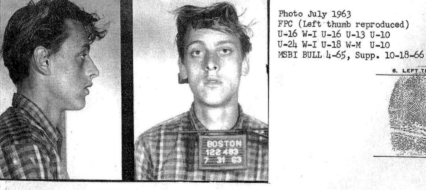

Photo July 1963
FPC (Left thumb reproduced)
U-16 W-I U-16 U-13 U-10
U-24 W-I U-18 W-M U-10
MSBI BULL 4-65, Supp. 10-18-66

6. LEFT THUMB

Murdered by William Geraway

MASSACHUSETTS DEPARTMENT OF PUBLIC SAFETY   CONFIDENTIAL POLICE BULLETIN

MURDER VICTIM: John B. O'NEILL, MBI 607353

GIST: Shot three times in back of head at Mickey Mouse Cafe, Revere Beach Parkway, Revere, along with Raymond DISTASIO, MBI 110979. Bodies discovered by the watchman at 5 P.M. on Nov. 15, 1965 when he arrived for work.

INVESTIGATING DEPARTMENTS: Revere PD and M.D.C. Police

DESCRIPTION: Born 3-19-39 in St. Albans, N. Y., 6', 147 lbs., lt. comp., parents, John & Anna O'Flaherty. (no further description)

ADDRESSES: 516 Revere Beach Blvd., Revere (at death)
22 Maple St., Littleton, N. H.
Whitfield, N. H.

OCCUPATIONS: Salesman, factory worker, technician

CRIMINAL RECORD: 1959 New Bedford Court, Speeding $15.00

ASSOCIATES:

ADDED INFORMATION: Apparent witness killed.

NO PRINTS OR PHOTO AVAILABLE
MSBI BULL 4-65, Supp. 10-18-66

Murdered by Joe Barboza and Nick Femia

MASSACHUSETTS DEPARTMENT OF PUBLIC SAFETY   CONFIDENTIAL POLICE BULLETIN

MURDER VICTIM: James J. McLEAN, alias "Buddy" McLEAN, MBI 188899, FBI 816627C,
US Marshal, Boston G-531, PD Boston 104498, Worcester HC 409,
MCI W-28904, Billerica HC 33045

GIST: Killed by shotgun blasts while sitting in a car in front of 300 Broadway,
Somerville on 10-30-65. With him in car at time of shooting and also
shot (but not killed) were Americo Sacramone, MBI 180855 and Anthony
D'Agostino, MBI 111418, (Sacramone is brother of Anthony D. Sacramone,
killed on 10-17-64)

INVESTIGATING DEPARTMENTS: Somerville P.D. and Mass. State Police

DESCRIPTION· Born 1-26-30 in Somerville, MW, 5'9", 190 lbs., brown hair, blue eyes,
med. comp., med build, parents, William & Dorothy (Guider), wife,
June (Kiley), 3 scars right forearm, appendix scar, Soc. Sec.
#018-22-3487

ADDRESSES: 3 Snow Terrace, Somerville (at death), 6 Otis St., Somerville, 20 Radcliffe Rd.,
Somerville, 25 Milford St., Charlestown, 254 Medford St., Charlestown

OCCUPATIONS: Longshoreman, truck driver, steam ship clerk, laborer

CRIMINAL RECORD: 1958 US Marshal, Boston, theft from interstate shipment, 1958 Boston PD
SP larceny over $100, 1962 Worc. H.C. A & B w/ dang. weapon &
wilful dest. of prop., 1962 MCI W-28904 A & B Dang. weap. 3-4 years

ASSOCIATES: Paul "Red" Brady, MBI 148238   Thomas J. Ballou, MBI 126357
Anthony D'Agostino, MBI 111418   Americo Sacramone, MBI 180855
Howard Winters, MBI 185640   Joseph Donahue, MBI 280339
William Winn, MBI 293988   Robert D. Kelley, MBI 187630

ADDED INFORMATION: Sacramone & D'Agostino were returned to Walpole as parole
violators on 11-17-65.

Photo May 1963
FPC (Rt. index reproduced)
U-15 W-I U-13 U-11 U-12
U-11 U-14 U-17 U-12 U-14
MSBI BULL 4-65, Supp. 10-18-66

2. R. FORE FINGER

MCI NORFOLK
15257
S 2 3 63

Murdered by Stevie Hughes

MASSACHUSETTS DEPARTMENT OF PUBLIC SAFETY   CONFIDENTIAL POLICE BULLETIN

MURDER VICTIM: Edward J. MCLAUGHLIN, alias "Punchy" MCLAUGHLIN, Edward AULD, MBI 44789, FBI 2747157, Boston 118532, PD Cambridge 7-328, PD Lynn 5420

GIST: Shot several times in the body at the Spring St. Metropolitan Transit Authority turn-around at VFW Parkway, West Roxbury on 10-20-65. Two men fled in gold Pontiac Convertible. Subject doing shooting described as 30 yrs., 5'9", med. build, crew haircut, wearing tortoise shell glasses.

INVESTIGATING DEPARTMENT: Boston Police Department

DESCRIPTION: Born 5-16-17 in Boston, MW, 5'10", 190 lbs., grey hair, hazel eyes, med. comp., med. build, parents, John & Annie (Clafferty), wife, Eleanor (Melody) upper left ear missing, right hand amputated, tattoos: eagle on chest with outspread wings; upper left arm, profile of woman smoking cigarette; left forearm, sailboat with 3 flying birds on each side; right forearm, flag.

ADDRESSES: 8 Ashdale Rd., Canton (at death); 7 Johnson Ave., Charlestown; 25 Monument Ave., Charlestown; 144 Main St., Charlestown; 16 Pond St., Jamaica Plain; Hotel DeSoto, Hot Springs, Ark.; 401 W. 44th St., Miami, Fla.

OCCUPATIONS: Union Delegate, Union Organizer, Laborer, Seaman, Longshoreman

CRIMINAL RECORD: PD Boston: 1931 Att. Larc. Auto, 1934 B & E & L, 1939 SP Robb. Unarmed, 1947 SP Armed Robb., 1951 Att Larceny, 1958 Vio. Auto Law, 1962 Larceny; PD Lynn: 1958 Larceny (3).

ASSOCIATES: George McLaughlin (Brother) MBI 122025   Harold R. Hannon (Victim) MBI 30350 Wilfred T. Delaney (Victim) MBI 147620   Leo C. Lowry (Victim) MBI 95215 Edward C. Deegan (Victim) MBI 129796

ADDED INFORMATION: This victim was shot on two previous occasions, on Nov. 24, 1964 on Beacon St., Brookline; and on Aug. 16, 1965 in Westwood.

Photo July 1962
FPC (Rt. thumb reproduced)
U-23 U-13 U-16 U-16 U-15
U-13 U-9 U-13 U-19 U-12
MSBI BULL 4-65, Supp. 10-18-66

Murdered by Stevie Flemmi

MASSACHUSETTS DEPARTMENT OF PUBLIC SAFETY   CONFIDENTIAL POLICE INFORMATION

MURDER VICTIM: Robert T. PALLADINO, alias Thomas R. PALLADINO, "Rocky" PALLADINO,
        MBI 352383, FBI 114154B, Somerville PD 4123, Medford PD D-17,
        Boston PD 114986, Newton PD 1755, MCI W-29136, SP Hawthorne NY 10339,
        USDB Cumberland, Pa. 14887

GIST: Body found on sidewalk on Beverly Street under Central Artery at rear of
      Anelex Building in the North End of Boston on 11-15-65. Shot in back of
      head and face bore the marks of a beating. Body appeared to have been
      dragged from a car to the spot where it was found.

INVESTIGATING DEPARTMENT: Boston Police Department

DESCRIPTION: Born 12-28-31 in Somerville, MW, 5'8", 170 lbs., brown hair & eyes,
      med. build, med. comp., parents, Anthony & Ethel (Beaudreau), wife,
      Geraldine (separated), tattoo of panther upper arm, 1" scar right cheek,
      1/2" scar on forehead over nose

ADDRESSES: 371 Main St., Winchester (at death)

OCCUPATIONS: Laborer, salesman, fruit peddler

CRIMINAL RECORD: 1952 SP Hawthorne NY escaped military prisoner (Air Force), USDB
      New Cumberland, Pa., Escapee 2-3 months, 1960 PD Somerville SP
      B & E (nt) & Larc., 1960 PD Medford B & E (dt), 1961 Newton Being
      Abroad Nt., poss. firearm w/o permit, poss. burg. tools, G.J. on
      all, 1962 MCI Walpole Robb. by force & violence, 5-7 yrs.

ASSOCIATES: Joseph M. Bochetti, MBI 345617   Bernard J. Zinna, MBI 107318

ADDED INFORMATION:

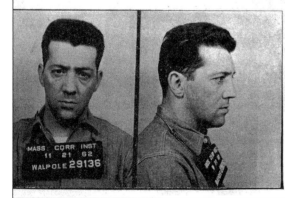

Photo November 1962
FPC (Rt. index reproduced)
W-O W-I W-I W-O U-15
W-M W-O W-I W-I U-16
MSBI BULL 4-65, Supp. 10-18-66

2. R. FORE FINGER

Murdered by John Martorano

MASSACHUSETTS DEPARTMENT OF PUBLIC SAFETY   CONFIDENTIAL POLICE BULLETIN

MURDER VICTIM: Raymond DiSTASIO, MBI 110979, MCI C-33231

GIST: Shot twice in back of head at Mickey Mouse Cafe, Revere Beach Parkway,
       Revere, along with John B. O'Neill, MBI 607353. Bodies discovered by
       the watchman at 5 PM on 11-15-65 when he arrived for work.

INVESTIGATING DEPARTMENTS: Revere PD and M.D.C. Police

DESCRIPTION: Born 1-3-30 in Boston, Mass., MW, 5'3½", 135 lbs., black hair, brown
              eyes, med. comp., parents, Raymond Ponzero & Grace F. (Nicosia).

ADDRESSES: 39 Prescott St., Medford (at death); 83 Bartlett Rd., Charlestown (1950)

OCCUPATIONS: Bartender, Novelty Stand Operator

CRIMINAL RECORD: Juvenile record for delinquency (B & E & L); transfer from
                  Shirley School to MCI Concord in 1946 & Norfolk Prison Colony
                  in 1946; paroled 9-12-47; good conduct discharge 6-12-50.

ASSOCIATES: Maxie Shackleford, MBI 282426, FBI 450423F

ADDED INFORMATION:

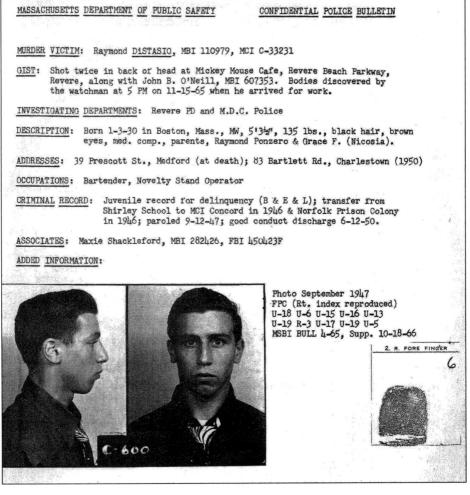

Photo September 1947
FPC (Rt. index reproduced)
U-18 U-6 U-15 U-16 U-13
U-19 R-3 U-17 U-19 U-5
MSBI BULL 4-65, Supp. 10-18-66

Murdered by Joe Barboza and Nick Femia

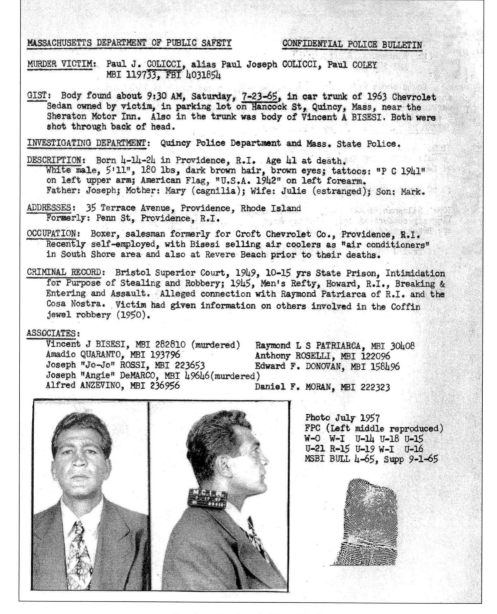

MASSACHUSETTS DEPARTMENT OF PUBLIC SAFETY   CONFIDENTIAL POLICE BULLETIN

MURDER VICTIM: Paul J. COLICCI, alias Paul Joseph COLICCI, Paul COLEY
       MBI 119733, FBI 4031854

GIST: Body found about 9:30 AM, Saturday, 7-23-65, in car trunk of 1963 Chevrolet
    Sedan owned by victim, in parking lot on Hancock St, Quincy, Mass, near the
    Sheraton Motor Inn. Also in the trunk was body of Vincent A BISESI. Both were
    shot through back of head.

INVESTIGATING DEPARTMENT: Quincy Police Department and Mass. State Police.

DESCRIPTION: Born 4-14-24 in Providence, R.I. Age 41 at death.
    White male, 5'11", 180 lbs, dark brown hair, brown eyes; tattoos: "P C 1941"
    on left upper arm; American Flag, "U.S.A. 1942" on left forearm.
    Father: Joseph; Mother: Mary (cagnilia); Wife: Julie (estranged); Son: Mark.

ADDRESSES: 35 Terrace Avenue, Providence, Rhode Island
    Formerly: Penn St, Providence, R.I.

OCCUPATION: Boxer, salesman formerly for Croft Chevrolet Co., Providence, R.I.
    Recently self-employed, with Bisesi selling air coolers as "air conditioners"
    in South Shore area and also at Revere Beach prior to their deaths.

CRIMINAL RECORD: Bristol Superior Court, 1949, 10-15 yrs State Prison, Intimidation
    for Purpose of Stealing and Robbery; 1945, Men's Refty, Howard, R.I., Breaking &
    Entering and Assault. Alleged connection with Raymond Patriarca of R.I. and the
    Cosa Nostra. Victim had given information on others involved in the Coffin
    jewel robbery (1950).

ASSOCIATES:
    Vincent J BISESI, MBI 282810 (murdered)   Raymond L S PATRIARCA, MBI 30408
    Amadio QUARANTO, MBI 193796   Anthony ROSELLI, MBI 122096
    Joseph "Jo-Jo" ROSSI, MBI 223653   Edward F. DONOVAN, MBI 158496
    Joseph "Angie" DeMARCO, MBI 49646 (murdered)
    Alfred ANZEVINO, MBI 236956
                              Daniel F. MORAN, MBI 222323

Photo July 1957
FPC (Left middle reproduced)
W-O W-I U-14 U-18 U-15
U-21 R-15 U-19 W-I U-16
MSBI BULL 4-65, Supp 9-1-65

Murdered by Rhode Island Mafia

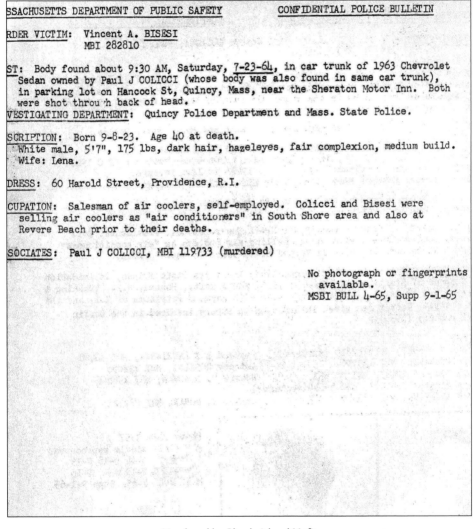

SSACHUSETTS DEPARTMENT OF PUBLIC SAFETY   CONFIDENTIAL POLICE BULLETIN

RDER VICTIM: Vincent A. BISESI
               MBI 282810

ST: Body found about 9:30 AM, Saturday, 7-23-64, in car trunk of 1963 Chevrolet
     Sedan owned by Paul J COLICCI (whose body was also found in same car trunk),
     in parking lot on Hancock St, Quincy, Mass, near the Sheraton Motor Inn. Both
     were shot throu h back of head.
VESTIGATING DEPARTMENT: Quincy Police Department and Mass. State Police.

SCRIPTION: Born 9-8-23. Age 40 at death.
     White male, 5'7", 175 lbs, dark hair, hazel eyes, fair complexion, medium build.
     Wife: Lena.

DRESS: 60 Harold Street, Providence, R.I.

CUPATION: Salesman of air coolers, self-employed. Colicci and Bisesi were
     selling air coolers as "air conditioners" in South Shore area and also at
     Revere Beach prior to their deaths.

SOCIATES: Paul J COLICCI, MBI 119733 (murdered)

                                        No photograph or fingerprints
                                          available.
                                        MSBI BULL 4-65, Supp 9-1-65

Murdered by Rhode Island Mafia

MASSACHUSETTS DEPART... .IT OF PUBLIC SAFETY   C...FIDENTIAL POLICE BULLETIN

MURDER VICTIM: Francis Regis BENJAMIN, alias Frank COTE, Frank H. Benjamin
           MBI 165443, FBI 988599A, Boston PD 108704 (1961), MCI-W 28573

GIST: Decapitated. Body found 4:15 PM, Monday, 5-4-64, outside of housing project
at 3 McDonough Way, South Boston, Mass, in trunk of 1963 Pontiac, no registration plates, reported stolen District 14, Boston Police Dept. Death due to
decapitation and bleeding; no other marks of violence. Medical Examiner esti-
mates date of death as 5-1-64 or 5-2-64.

INVESTIGATING DEPARTMENT: Boston Police Department.

DESCRIPTION: Born 12-19-30 or 12-10-32 in Pawtucket, R.I. Age 32 (?) at death.
Male white, 5'10", 165 lbs, blond hair, blue eyes, slim build, medium comp.
Tattoos: Bird with banner and Name "Shirley" right upper arm; heart with piercing
dagger and names "Frankie", "Shirley", American Flag and "U.S.A." on left upper
arm; dangling hearts below banner on chest; initials "S.B." on left side, initials
"D.B." on right side; scar from appendectomy; 1-inch scar below right eye.
Father: Leslie; Mother: Gertrude (Donnelly); Wife: Shirley (Gadbout).

ADDRESSES: 5 Norwell St, Dorchester (at death)
Previously lived in Roxbury

OCCUPATIONS: Press operator 1956; roofer and laborer since that time.

CRIMINAL RECORD: 1953 State Penty, Jefferson City, Mo., Robbery 1st Degree, 5 yrs;
1957 MCI Walpole, Robbery Being Armed, 5-7 yrs (paroled 9-1-59); 9-26-61 MCI
Walpole, Robbery Being Armed, 5-8 yrs (paroled 4-20-64, exp. 1-15-68). Also
in 1951 had served 30 days County Jail, Bridgeport, Conn, for Breaking & Entering.

ASSOCIATES:
Thomas J BALLOU, MBI 126357   James FAHERTY, MBI 26214

ADDED INFORMATION: Victim was close associate of James FAHERTY. Faherty is presently
serving a sentence at MCI Walpole for the Brink's Express holdup. It is alleged
that Benjamin was going to even the score with Harold HANNON for James FAHERTY.
About 11:00 PM, Saturday, 4-25-64, Benjamin was observed in the company of
Thomas J BALLOU at the corner of Bowdoin and Washington Streets, Dorchester, Mass.

Photo April 1964
FPC (Rt middle reproduced)
U-9 W-I W-I W-O U-16
U-10 W-O W-O W-I U-16
MSBI BULL 4-65, Supp 9-1-65

Murdered by Wimpy Bennet and Jimmy Flemmi

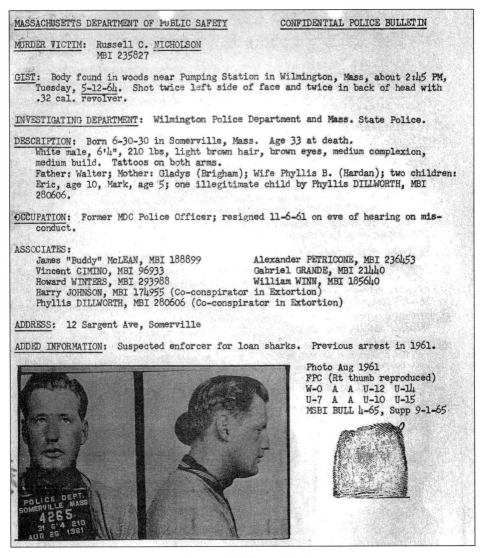

MASSACHUSETTS DEPARTMENT OF PUBLIC SAFETY   CONFIDENTIAL POLICE BULLETIN

MURDER VICTIM: Russell C. NICHOLSON
                MBI 235827

GIST: Body found in woods near Pumping Station in Wilmington, Mass, about 2:45 PM,
       Tuesday, 5-12-64. Shot twice left side of face and twice in back of head with
       .32 cal. revolver.

INVESTIGATING DEPARTMENT: Wilmington Police Department and Mass. State Police.

DESCRIPTION: Born 6-30-30 in Somerville, Mass. Age 33 at death.
       White male, 6'4", 210 lbs, light brown hair, brown eyes, medium complexion,
       medium build. Tattoos on both arms.
       Father: Walter; Mother: Gladys (Brigham); Wife Phyllis B. (Hardan); two children:
       Eric, age 10, Mark, age 5; one illegitimate child by Phyllis DILLWORTH, MBI
       280606.

OCCUPATION: Former MDC Police Officer; resigned 11-6-61 on eve of hearing on mis-
       conduct.

ASSOCIATES:
       James "Buddy" McLEAN, MBI 188899   Alexander PETRICONE, MBI 236453
       Vincent CIMINO, MBI 96933   Gabriel GRANDE, MBI 21440
       Howard WINTERS, MBI 293988   William WINN, MBI 185640
       Harry JOHNSON, MBI 174955 (Co-conspirator in Extortion)
       Phyllis DILLWORTH, MBI 280606 (Co-conspirator in Extortion)

ADDRESS: 12 Sargent Ave, Somerville

ADDED INFORMATION: Suspected enforcer for loan sharks. Previous arrest in 1961.

Photo Aug 1961
FPC (Rt thumb reproduced)
W-O A   A   U-12 U-14
U-7 A   A   U-10 U-15
MSBI BULL 4-65, Supp 9-1-65

Murder officially unsolved

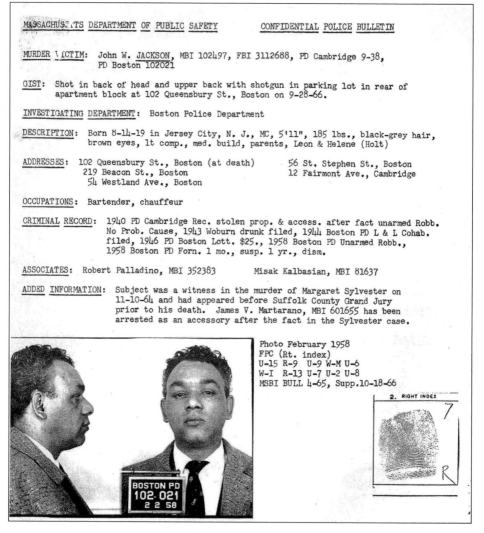

MASSACHUSETTS DEPARTMENT OF PUBLIC SAFETY   CONFIDENTIAL POLICE BULLETIN

MURDER VICTIM: John W. JACKSON, MBI 102497, FBI 3112688, PD Cambridge 9-38,
                 PD Boston 102021

GIST: Shot in back of head and upper back with shotgun in parking lot in rear of
        apartment block at 102 Queensbury St., Boston on 9-28-66.

INVESTIGATING DEPARTMENT: Boston Police Department

DESCRIPTION: Born 8-14-19 in Jersey City, N. J., MC, 5'11", 185 lbs., black-grey hair,
               brown eyes, lt comp., med. build, parents, Leon & Helene (Holt)

ADDRESSES: 102 Queensbury St., Boston (at death)   56 St. Stephen St., Boston
             219 Beacon St., Boston   12 Fairmont Ave., Cambridge
             54 Westland Ave., Boston

OCCUPATIONS: Bartender, chauffeur

CRIMINAL RECORD: 1940 PD Cambridge Rec. stolen prop. & access. after fact unarmed Robb.
                   No Prob. Cause, 1943 Woburn drunk filed, 1944 Boston PD L & L Cohab.
                   filed, 1946 PD Boston Lott. $25., 1958 Boston PD Unarmed Robb.,
                   1958 Boston PD Forn. 1 mo., susp. 1 yr., dism.

ASSOCIATES: Robert Palladino, MBI 352383   Misak Kalbasian, MBI 81637

ADDED INFORMATION: Subject was a witness in the murder of Margaret Sylvester on
                     11-10-64 and had appeared before Suffolk County Grand Jury
                     prior to his death. James V. Martarano, MBI 601655 has been
                     arrested as an accessory after the fact in the Sylvester case.

Photo February 1958
FPC (Rt. index)
U-15 R-9 U-9 W-M U-6
W-I R-13 U-7 U-2 U-8
MSBI BULL 4-65, Supp.10-18-66

2. RIGHT INDEX

BOSTON PD
102-021
2 2 58

Murdered by John Martorano

MASSACHUSETTS DEPARTMENT OF PUBLIC SAFETY   CONFIDENTIAL POLICE BULLETIN

MURDER VICTIM: Samuel O. LINDENBAUM, Alias Samuel LINDEN, Leonard YOUNG,
                Samuel LINDENSON, Samuel LINDENBON, Samuel LINDERSON, Samuel LUNDEN,
                Sammy LEONARD, Sam KAUFMAN, MBI 11806, FBI 554895, Billerica HC 29655,
                PD Boston 101789, SP 24801, PD Medford B-8, SP 20261, DIHC 39861,
                E. Cambridge HC 90780, Suff. Co. J1. 7042

GIST: Shot in car on Route 114 in Middleton in the area of the Three Pines
       Restaurant on 9-23-66 by a high-powered rifle using armor piercing shells,
       and fired from a passing car. Also in the car and killed at the same time,
       was Stephen Hughes, MBI 111639. A loaded .38 cal. revolver and a quantity
       of policy slips (lottery) were found in the car.

INVESTIGATING DEPARTMENTS: Middleton PD and Mass. State Police

DESCRIPTION: Born 1-18-99 in Russia, MW, 5'2", 167 lbs., gray hair, brown eyes, med. com
              heavy build, parents, Isaac & Ida (Libberburg), wife, Bertha (div.)

ADDRESSES: 405 Broadway, Revere (at death)   178 Second St., Chelsea
            12 Maverick St., Chelsea   17 Arch Ave., Haverhill
            260 Washington Ave., Chelsea   20 Cortes St., Boston
            36 West Newton St., Boston   26 Arlington Ave., Revere
            Hotel Manger, Boston   Hotel Bradford, Boston
            203 Park Drive, Boston   19 Dolphin Ave., Revere
            31 Dolphin Ave., Revere

OCCUPATIONS: Paper Boy, plumber, boxer, laborer, business man, trucker,
              upholsterer, iron worker

CRIMINAL RECORD: 1914 DIHC B&E, Prob., 1920 E. Cambridge HC L & L Cohab. $100.,
                  1925 Haverhill PD Robb. & Lewd. 7-10 yrs. & $10., 1925 MSP Robb.
                  7-10 yrs., 1932 PD Boston SP Aiding & Abetting prisoner to escape,
                  1935 SP Topsfield, SP Armed Robb. & Rec. Stolen Goods, 1936 DIHC
                  Oper. after lic. rev. & L & L Cohab. 6-3 mos., 1937 Asslt. w/intent
                  to Rob 15-20 yrs., 1951 PD Boston SP Robb., 1951 PD Revere Abortion,
                  1952 MSP Abortion 4-6 yrs., 1958 SP B & E (nt), 1959 Billerica HC
                  Poss. Burg. Imp. 1 yr.

ASSOCIATES: Stephen Hughes, MBI 111639 (victim)   Peter J. DiNatale, MBI 33345

ADDED INFORMATION:

Photo October 1959
FPC (Left thumb reproduced)
U-18 U-13 W-M W-O U-17
U-I W-O U-15 W-I U-12
MSBI BULL 4-65, Supp. 10-18-66

6. Left Thumb

Murdered by Winter Hill

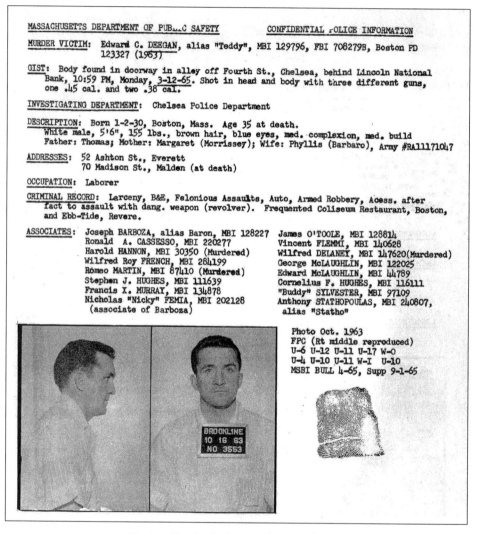

MASSACHUSETTS DEPARTMENT OF PUBLIC SAFETY   CONFIDENTIAL POLICE INFORMATION

MURDER VICTIM: Edward C. DEEGAN, alias "Teddy", MBI 129796, FBI 708279B, Boston PD
123327 (1963)

GIST: Body found in doorway in alley off Fourth St., Chelsea, behind Lincoln National
Bank, 10:59 PM, Monday, 3-12-65. Shot in head and body with three different guns,
one .45 cal. and two .38 cal.

INVESTIGATING DEPARTMENT: Chelsea Police Department

DESCRIPTION: Born 1-2-30, Boston, Mass. Age 35 at death.
White male, 5'6", 155 lbs., brown hair, blue eyes, med. complexion, med. build
Father: Thomas; Mother: Margaret (Morrissey); Wife: Phyllis (Barbaro), Army #RA11171047

ADDRESSES: 52 Ashton St., Everett
70 Madison St., Malden (at death)

OCCUPATION: Laborer

CRIMINAL RECORD: Larceny, B&E, Felonious Assaults, Auto, Armed Robbery, Acess. after
fact to assault with dang. weapon (revolver). Frequented Coliseum Restaurant, Boston,
and Ebb-Tide, Revere.

ASSOCIATES: Joseph BARBOZA, alias Baron, MBI 128227   James O'TOOLE, MBI 128814
Ronald A. CASSESSO, MBI 220277   Vincent FLEMMI, MBI 140628
Harold HANNON, MBI 30350 (Murdered)   Wilfred DELANEY, MBI 147620(Murdered)
Wilfred Roy FRENCH, MBI 284199   George McLAUGHLIN, MBI 122025
Romeo MARTIN, MBI 87410 (Murdered)   Edward McLAUGHLIN, MBI 44789
Stephen J. HUGHES, MBI 111639   Cornelius F. HUGHES, MBI 116111
Francis X. MURRAY, MBI 134878   "Buddy" SYLVESTER, MBI 97109
Nicholas "Nicky" FEMIA, MBI 202128   Anthony STATHOPOULAS, MBI 240807,
(associate of Barboza)   alias "Statho"

Photo Oct. 1963
FPC (Rt middle reproduced)
U-6 U-12 U-11 U-17 W-O
U-4 U-10 U-11 W-I U-10
MSBI BULL 4-65, Supp 9-1-65

BROOKLINE
10 16 63
NO 3553

Murdered by Joe Barboza and Jimmy Flemmi

MASSACHUSETTS DEPARTMENT OF PUBLIC SAFETY   CONFIDENTIAL POLICE INFORMATION

MURDER VICTIM: John BARBIERI, Jr., alias, John SANTIGARDO, John SANTIAGO, John
STANLIANO, Harry PATTON, Frank DEASY, John MURRAY, Bob MORAN,
"Jew", "Heeb", MBI 151393, Boston PD 59632(1942)

GIST: Body found in woods about 230 feet off Carpenter St., Rehoboth, Mass., 50
feet from vehicle, RI Reg. SE220, about 10:40 AM, Tuesday, 3-2-65. Death
caused by gunshot at close range, entered back of left ear and exited left
eye.

INVESTIGATING DEPARTMENT: Rehoboth Police Department and Mass. State Police

DESCRIPTION: Born 11-6-17, 11-6-14 or 11-6-12, Mamaroneck, N.Y.
White male, 5'11", 180 lbs., dark chestnut hair, brown eyes, med. build
Wife: Beatrice; two children, names unknown; Daughter: Jean (used her car
when he left Rhode Island)

ADDRESSES: 295 Cedar Lane, East Greenwich, R.I. ($65,000. ranch)
45 Coyle St., Warwick, R.I. (1942)

OCCUPATION: Self-operated small sewing machine business; previously carpenter,
contractor.

CRIMINAL RECORD: Arrested 1942 on warrant charging larceny (value $119.), dis-
missed for want of prosecution; possible link to hi-jack operation in Providence, R.I. area. Known fence, possible tail-
gater. On bail for having stolen car in possession (stolen in
Washington, D.C.)

ASSOCIATES: Gerard T. OUIMETTE, MBI 193697
Kenneth KNOWLES, MBI 91149
Joseph OSTIGUY, MBI 223033

Photo Apr. 1942
FPC (Lft thumb reproduced)
W-O W-O W-O W-M U-15
W-I U13 U-17 W-I W-I
MSBI BULL 4-65, Supp 9-1-65

BOSTON POLICE
59632
4 16 42

Murder unsolved

MASSACHUSETTS DEPARTMENT OF PUBLIC SAFETY   CONFIDENTIAL POLICE INFORMATION

MURDER VICTIM: Cornelius HUGHES, alias Cornelius Francis HUGHES, "Connie" HUGHES,
               MBI 116111, FBI 5040762, PD Boston 108046 DIHC 12324-5,
               PD Chelsea 2128, PD Cambridge 7-443, PD Somerville 2873,
               MR Concord 34244, MSP 23696

GIST: Shot with high-powered rifle on Northeast Expressway in Revere in his car on
      5-25-66. Car and body found by passing motorist who thought there had been
      an accident and notified MDC Police.

INVESTIGATING DEPARTMENTS: Revere PD and M.D.C. Police

DESCRIPTION: Born 7-13-29 in Boston, MW, 5'9", 190 lbs., chest. hair, blue eyes,
             med. comp., med. build, parents, Stephen & Mary (Gearin), wife,
             Marion (Fitzpatrick), scar right side lip, tattoo, left wrist "Janie"

ADDRESSES: 12 Hancock Rd., Malden (at death)   40 Allston St., Charlestown
            2 Carney St., Charlestown   131 Grove St., West Roxbury
          377 Bunker Hill St., Charlestown   405 Lynn St., Malden

OCCUPATIONS: Laborer, longshoreman, truck driver, electrician's helper

CRIMINAL RECORD: PD Boston: 1947 SP Larc. Auto, 1948 SP Armed Robb., 1953 SP A & B
                 Dang. Weap. (no bill), 1954 SP Armed Robb. (rel.), 1956 SP B & E
                 Bldg. (nt), 1956 SP Robb., 1959 SP Larc. MV; SP Charlestown 1948 A & B
                 w/int. to Rob (armed), A & B w/ dang. weap., unlawful carrying weap.
                 on person, 5-7 yrs., 5-7 yrs., conc. 3-5 yrs. conc., Mass. Refty. 1948
                 transfer from SP), 1954 Cambridge PD SP Armed Robb., 1955 PD Chelsea
                 Larc. (2) 4 mos. on each, DIHC Larc. (2) 4-4 mos.

ASSOCIATES: Stephen Hughes (brother) MBI 111639 (victim)
            Theodore Deegan, MBI 129796

ADDED INFORMATION:

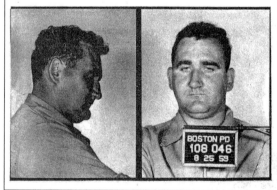

Photo October 1959
FPC (Rt. thumb reproduced)
U-17 U-6 U-4 U-14 U-13
U-18 R-7 U-11 U-11 U-12
MSBI BULL 4-65, Supp. 10-18-66

1. RIGHT THUMB.

Murdered by Winter Hill

MASSACHUSETTS DEPARTMENT OF PUBLIC SAFETY   CONFIDENTIAL POLICE INFORMATION

MURDER VICTIM: Anthony VERANIS, alias "Tony" VERANIS, Anthony VERONIS,
                Anthony VERARIES, MBI 178926, FBI 346871C, PD Boston 123652,
                MCI SH-7480, MCI W-27833

GIST: Body found at the foot of an embankment off Route 28 in Quincy on 4-26-66.
       Shot in head with head and face badly battered. It is believed subject was
       slain elsewhere and body dumped at this location. A blood-soaked coat was
       found on top of the embankment. Body found by former marathoner during
       early morning run. Subject seen with Victim Sidlauskas on night of 4-23-66.

INVESTIGATING DEPARTMENTS: Quincy PD and Mass. State Police

DESCRIPTION: Born 6-20-38 in Boston, MW, 5'8", 155 lbs., chest. hair, blue eyes,
              med. build, med. comp., parents, Anthony & Theresa (Dillon), tattoos:
              boxer with "Tony" on left arm, "Luck" right fingers, "TONY" left
              fingers, deformed nose, partial upper plate.

ADDRESSES: 691 Washington St., Dorchester (at death)
            1086 Dorchester Ave., Dorchester

OCCUPATIONS: Laborer, longshoreman, boxer

CRIMINAL RECORD: 1956 Boston PD SP A & B dang. weap., 1959 Boston PD SP A & B dang.
                  weap. 3 yrs. prob., 1960 PD Boston SP Unarmed Robb. 2½-3 yrs.,
                  1960 Walpole Robb. 2-3 yrs., Paroled 1961, 1961 Boston PD SP B & E
                  (nt), 1961 MCI Bridgewater SH B & E (nt) w/intent to commit larc.,
                  A & B on P.O., Wanton injury to property, 1963 Boston PD SP B & E
                  (nt) 2½-5 yrs., 1963 Paroled, 1964 Ret'd Walpole, 1965 Paroled.

ASSOCIATES: David H. Sidlauskas, MBI 272147 (victim)

ADDED INFORMATION:

Photo March 1965
FPC (Rt. thumb reproduced)
W-O R-9 U-11 W-M W-O
U-16 U-12 U-11 U-12 U-13
MSBI BULL 4-65

Murdered by John Martorano

MASSACHUSETTS DEPARTMENT OF PUBLIC SAFETY   CONFIDENTIAL POLICE BULLETIN

MURDER VICTIM: Henry F. REDDINGTON, alias Henry BUCKLEY, John T. VOGEL
    MBI 120554, FBI 62158A, Boston PD 122352

GIST: Body found about 3:17 AM, Saturday, 1-23-65, in the office of Ab-Wey
    Realty, 1595 Main St, Weymouth (victim was owner). Death caused by
    three .38 cal. wounds in chest and three .38 cal. wounds in head.

INVESTIGATING DEPARTMENT: Weymouth Police Department and Mass. State Police.

DESCRIPTION: Born 11-12-13 in Boston, Mass. Age 51 at death.
    White male, 5'9", 210 lbs, dark brown hair, blue eyes, stocky build, small
    scar center of forehead, wart right side of nose.
    Father: Malachi J.; Mother: Margaret (Hamrock); Wife: Marie (Hebert);
    Daughter: Margaret A. Fletcher, 66D Reuben James St, Acia, Hawaii

OCCUPATION: Real estate operator, bartender, truck business, laundry & livery
    service.

ADDRESSES: 1595 Main St, Weymouth (at death)   650 Dudley St, Roxbury
    21 Wood St, Milton   38 Lancaster St, Braintree
    115 Blue Hill Road, Milton

CRIMINAL RECORD: 1953 State Prison, Contraband to Convict (Letters and Benzadrine
    to Andrew VOLIANITES in State Prison), 2½-3 yrs & 2½-3 yrs from and after;
    1954 Federal conviction Violation Wagering Tax Law, 6 mos after state sentence;
    1956 Federal conviction Dyer Act, Interstate Transportation Stolen Motor Vehicle,
    5 yrs after state sentence with a 2 yr sentence concurrent; victim was suspected
    of providing concealment for wanted persons, and of arson in Milton.

ASSOCIATES: Edward S JOHNSON, MBI 88453   Dorothy BARSHARD, MBI 177224
    Andrew VOLIANITES, MBI 131274   John J ARQUILLA, MBI 356016
    Theodore VOLIANITES, MBI 144571   Gerard H PRESUTTI, MBI 347609
    Frank James CAMPBELL, MBI 204008   James S O'TOOLE, MBI 128814
    Joseph "Mad Dog" DONOHUE, MBI 280339   John RICE, MBI 119429
    Vincent DiSANGRO, MBI 183406   Raffiaele MAZZUCCO, MBI 354316
    Paul DiSANGRO, MBI 240226   William J McARDLE, MBI 66251

Photo July 1963
FPC (Right thumb reproduced)
W-O W-I U-9 W-M W-O
U-18 W-O U-13 W-I U-15
Ref right little & left ring
    as U
MSBI BULL 4-65, Supp 9-1-65

Murdered by Spike O'Toole

MASSACHUSETTS DEPARTMENT OF PU_LIC SAFETY   CONFIDENTIAL POLICE INFORMATION

MURDER VICTIM: Joseph Ralph FRANCIONE, alias "Jake", "Big Jack"
    MBI 117568, FBI 384206A, Boston PD 122762 (1964), MCI W-28117

GIST: Shot at 49 South Avenue, Revere, 2:30 PM, Monday, 1-25-65. Three shots
    through back of head by .38 cal. weapon. Body found face down on kitchen
    floor. Seen shoveling snow at 2:00 PM by landlord.

INVESTIGATING DEPARTMENT: Revere Police Department and Mass. State Police

DESCRIPTION: Born 2-5-29 Boston, Mass. Age 39 at death.
    White male, 6'1", 185 lbs., black hair, brown eyes, medium complexion.
    Tattoo right upper arm: cross, "In memory of father"; 4" ulcer operation scar
    stomach; Soc.Sec.No. 030-20-5057; Army No. 11077697
    Father: Ralph; Mother: Esther (Rotondi); Wife: Theresa (Lopilato), divorced,
    she was known as Nancy Hill, MBI 291730, bad checks and contempts for false
    name, husband made restitution. Two children. Another wife given as: Emma
    (DiCicco) from 1949-59. Sister: Mrs. Louise N. Boschetto, 73 Neponset Ave.,
    Hyde Park.

ADDRESSES: 49 South Ave., Revere (at death); landlord: Angelo Vaiarella
    Moved from Watertown about 1 year ago; 103 Edenfield Ave., Watertown
    121 Broadsound Lane, Revere (1963)   16 Greenough Lane, Boston (1950)
    58 Salem St., Boston (1960)   41 Bowdoin St., Boston (1949)
    39 Salutation St., Boston (1950-55)   38 Leverett St., Boston (1949)

OCCUPATION: "International Public Relations", 350 W. 55th St., New York, N.Y.
    William J. Smith, Jr., 154 Norwich St., Hartford, Conn.
    Also, laborer, salesman, baker, painter, shipper, presser, peddler.

CRIMINAL RECORD: 1953 Mass. State Prison, Larceny from person; 1960 MCI Walpole
    Brk & Ent Bldg; 1962 Middlesex Co. H.C., Rec. Stolen Goods; 1964 on bail, fur
    larceny Boston; suspect fur robberies and jewelry burglaries; bad checks Med-
    ford 1962-63; Non-support 1964; suspected of selling stolen cars. Asslt &
    Batt on Barney VILLANI, MBI 199850, 1958.

ASSOCIATES:
    Robert DONATI, MBI 219208 (aka "Iozza")   Anthony J. ZIRPOLO, MBI 346042
    George McLAUGHLIN, MBI 122025   (possible relative suggested:
    Joseph V PUZZANGARA, MBI 130817   Joseph J. ZIRPOLO, MBI 201681)
    Thomas D. TIMMONS, MBI 69284   Frederick LATORELLA, MBI 95841(murdered)
    James SACCOACH, MBI 130698   Henry CIPRIANO, MBI 138104
    Samuel LINDEN, aka LINDENBAUM, MBI 11806   James F. COYNE, MBI 276821
    Joseph DeMARCO, MBI 49646 (murdered)   Robert JOYNT, MBI 129507(who was associate
    Thomas F. ROSSI, MBI 200241   of Peter CASSETTA, MBI 140057, Murdered)
    Bartholomew VILLANI, MBI 199850

ADDED INFORMATION: Frequented Ebb-Tide, Revere Beach. Used 1964 Ford Conv., L89-082
    reg. to Clara B. LOMBARDO, 183 Malden St., Revere. In debt to loan sharks.

Photo Dec. 1961
FPC (Rt thumb reproduced)
U-21 U-9 U-12 U-17 U-12
U-14 W-M U-12 U-14 U-9
MSBI BULL 4-65, Supp 9-1-65

Murdered by Joe Barboza

MASSACHUSETTS DEPARTMENT OF PUBLIC SAFETY   CONFIDENTIAL POLICE INFORMATION

MURDER VICTIM: Rocco DISEGLIO, alias Rocco DESIGLIO, Rocco DISEGLEO, Rocco DISIGLIO, Rocco SEGLIO, "Rocky" DISIGLIO, MBI 183014, FBI 612548C, Middx. Co. HC 139187, Billerica HC 26730, PD Watertown 2007

GIST: Body found in car parked in wooded section off Rowley Bridge St., Topsfield on 6-16-66 by State Trooper after tip by Boston Police. Bullet hole in back of subject's head. Victim's car was Thurderbird Sedan, Mass. Reg. R34-822.

INVESTIGATING DEPARTMENTS: Topsfield PD and Mass. State Police

DESCRIPTION: Born 4-11-39 in Italy, MW, 5'7½", 147 lbs., dark brown hair, brown eyes, med. build, dark comp., parents, Salvatore & Concetta (DeSantis), wife, Joanne; Tattoos: "Rocco" & woman on right arm, playing card spade on back of left hand, "X" on left hand; scar on left wrist.

ADDRESSES: West St., Newton (at death)   364 Watertown St., Newton
           145 Riverview Ave., Waltham   369 Watertown St., Newton
            17 Dalby St., Newton   52 Clyde St., Newtonville

OCCUPATIONS: Boxer, laborer

CRIMINAL RECORD: 1957 PD Newton, A & B, 6 mos. HC, 1957 E. Cambridge HC A & B 6 mos., 1961 PD Watertown Poss. Burg. Tools & Att. B & E (nt), Prob. 6 yrs. on each, 1962 Waltham Court Larc. under false pret., filed, 1962 Newton Court Gaming Pub. Place, filed, 1963 Middx. Sup. Crt. Larc. (7), Larc. (3), Burg. Imp. in Poss., Prob. 2 yrs., Prob. 2 yrs., 5 yrs. 1 day MCI Concord, susp. prob. 5-22-67, 1963 Middx. Sup. Crt. Att. B & E (nt), prob. 5-22-67.

ASSOCIATES: Robert A. Ciolfi, MBI 218547   Joseph DeNucci, MBI 210875

ADDED INFORMATION:

Photo February 1961
FPC (Rt. middle reproduced)
U-19 U-18 U-6 U-19 U-12
W-I W-O U-14 U-16 U-11
MSBI BULL 4-65, Supp. 10-18-66

3. Right Middle Finger

Murdered by the Boston Mafia

MASSACHUSETTS DEPARTMENT OF PUBLIC SAFETY   CONFIDENTIAL POLICE BULLETIN

MURDER VICTIM: Stephen HUGHES, alias Stephen R. HUGHES, Stephen Joseph HUGHES, Steve
               HUGHES, MBI 111639, FBI 4724544, U.S. Marshal, Boston 2126, MCI W-27983
               Boston PD 97216, PD Cambridge 7-444, DIHC 90714, Billerica HC 20104

GIST: Shot in car on Route 114 in Middleton in the area of the Three Pines Restaurant
       on 9-23-66 by a high-powered rifle using armor piercing shells fired from a
       passing car. Also in the car and killed at the same time was Samuel LINDENBAUM,
       MBI 11806. A loaded .38 cal. revolver and a quantity of policy slips (lottery)
       were found in the car.

INVESTIGATING DEPARTMENTS: Middleton PD and Mass. State Police

DESCRIPTION: Born 7-23-27 in Boston, MW, 5'9", 210 lbs., brown hair, hazel eyes,
             med. comp., stocky build, parents, Stephen J. & Mary (Gearin),
             wife, Eleanor (Selig), faint scar left elbow, two scars left shin.

ADDRESSES: 105 Bunker Hill St., Charlestown   2 Carney Court, Charlestown
            40 Allston St., Charlestown

OCCUPATIONS: Laborer, longshoreman

CRIMINAL RECORD: PD Boston: 1946 Larc. of Auto, 1947 SP Larc. Auto, NG, Oper. w/o
                 Lic. Filed, Using w/o Auth., Conc. Refty., susp., 2 yrs. prob.,
                 1948 A & B on P. O., 1950 SP Armed Robb., 1956 SP B & E; 1947 Somerville
                 PD SP Larc. Auto, 1948 PD Arlington Unloaded Revolver in motor vehicle
                 2 yrs. susp., 1950 Billerica HC Larc. Auto, Poss. Dang. Weapon, Poss.
                 Firearm, Consp. (4) 18 mos. (4 conc.); 1954 PD Cambridge SP Robb.
                 1960 MCI Walpole Being Armed with dang. weap. did asslt. with intent to
                 murder, 5-7 yrs., 1965 US Marshal, Boston Rec. stolen goods, inter-
                 state, 10 mos. app., 1965 State Police Boston, Larc. over $100.00.

ASSOCIATES: Cornelius Hughes (brother-victim), MBI 116111
            Samuel Lindenbaum (victim), MBI 11806
            Daniel J. McCarthy, MBI 54397
            Fred Zoboli, MBI 117765

ADDED INFORMATION:

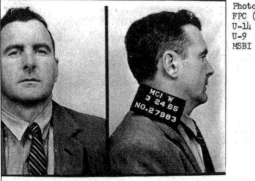

Photo, March 1965
FPC (Rt. index reproduced)
U-14 U-3 A   U-7 U-17
U-9 T   R-4 U-16 U-15
MSBI BULL 4-65, Supp. 10-18-66

Murdered by Winter Hill

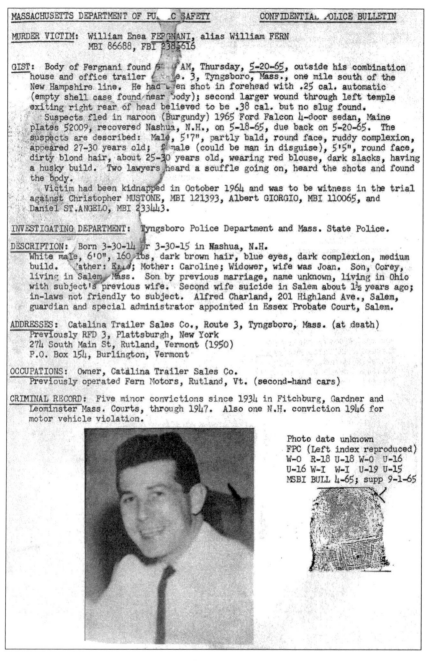

MASSACHUSETTS DEPARTMENT OF PU C SAFETY   CONFIDENTIAL POLICE BULLETIN

MURDER VICTIM: William Enea FERGNANI, alias William FERN
                MBI 86688, FBI 2383516

GIST: Body of Fergnani found 5 AM, Thursday, 5-20-65, outside his combination
       house and office trailer   e. 3, Tyngsboro, Mass., one mile south of the
       New Hampshire line. He had en shot in forehead with .25 cal. automatic
       (empty shell case found near body); second larger wound through left temple
       exiting right rear of head believed to be .38 cal. but no slug found.
         Suspects fled in maroon (Burgundy) 1965 Ford Falcon 4-door sedan, Maine
       plates 52009, recovered Nashua, N.H., on 5-18-65, due back on 5-20-65. The
       suspects are described: Male, 5'7", partly bald, round face, ruddy complexion,
       appeared 27-30 years old; female (could be man in disguise), 5'5", round face,
       dirty blond hair, about 25-30 years old, wearing red blouse, dark slacks, having
       a husky build. Two lawyers heard a scuffle going on, heard the shots and found
       the body.
         Victim had been kidnapped in October 1964 and was to be witness in the trial
       against Christopher MUSTONE, MBI 121393, Albert GIORGIO, MBI 110065, and
       Daniel ST.ANGELO, MBI 233443.

INVESTIGATING DEPARTMENT: Tyngsboro Police Department and Mass. State Police.

DESCRIPTION: Born 3-30-14 or 3-30-15 in Nashua, N.H.
       White male, 6'0", 160 lbs, dark brown hair, blue eyes, dark complexion, medium
       build.   Father: E   ; Mother: Caroline; Widower, wife was Joan. Son, Corey,
       living in Salem, Mass. Son by previous marriage, name unknown, living in Ohio
       with subject's previous wife. Second wife suicide in Salem about 1½ years ago;
       in-laws not friendly to subject. Alfred Charland, 201 Highland Ave., Salem,
       guardian and special administrator appointed in Essex Probate Court, Salem.

ADDRESSES: Catalina Trailer Sales Co., Route 3, Tyngsboro, Mass. (at death)
       Previously RFD 3, Plattsburgh, New York
       274 South Main St, Rutland, Vermont (1950)
       P.O. Box 154, Burlington, Vermont

OCCUPATIONS: Owner, Catalina Trailer Sales Co.
       Previously operated Fern Motors, Rutland, Vt. (second-hand cars)

CRIMINAL RECORD: Five minor convictions since 1934 in Fitchburg, Gardner and
       Leominster Mass. Courts, through 1947. Also one N.H. conviction 1946 for
       motor vehicle violation.

Photo date unknown
FPC (Left index reproduced)
W-O R-18 U-18 W-O U-16
U-16 W-I W-I U-19 U-15
MSBI BULL 4-65; supp 9-1-65

Murder unsolved

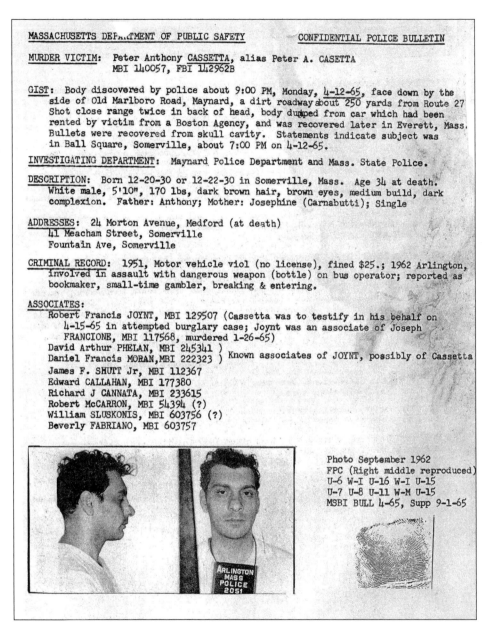

MASSACHUSETTS DEPARTMENT OF PUBLIC SAFETY   CONFIDENTIAL POLICE BULLETIN

MURDER VICTIM: Peter Anthony CASSETTA, alias Peter A. CASETTA
                MBI 140057, FBI 142962B

GIST: Body discovered by police about 9:00 PM, Monday, 4-12-65, face down by the
       side of Old Marlboro Road, Maynard, a dirt roadway about 250 yards from Route 27
       Shot close range twice in back of head, body dumped from car which had been
       rented by victim from a Boston Agency, and was recovered later in Everett, Mass.
       Bullets were recovered from skull cavity. Statements indicate subject was
       in Ball Square, Somerville, about 7:00 PM on 4-12-65.

INVESTIGATING DEPARTMENT: Maynard Police Department and Mass. State Police.

DESCRIPTION: Born 12-20-30 or 12-22-30 in Somerville, Mass. Age 34 at death.
       White male, 5'10", 170 lbs, dark brown hair, brown eyes, medium build, dark
       complexion. Father: Anthony; Mother: Josephine (Carnabutti); Single

ADDRESSES: 24 Morton Avenue, Medford (at death)
       41 Meacham Street, Somerville
       Fountain Ave, Somerville

CRIMINAL RECORD: 1951, Motor vehicle viol (no license), fined $25.; 1962 Arlington,
       involved in assault with dangerous weapon (bottle) on bus operator; reported as
       bookmaker, small-time gambler, breaking & entering.

ASSOCIATES:
       Robert Francis JOYNT, MBI 129507 (Cassetta was to testify in his behalf on
          4-15-65 in attempted burglary case; Joynt was an associate of Joseph
          FRANCIONE, MBI 117568, murdered 1-26-65)
       David Arthur PHELAN, MBI 245341)
       Daniel Francis MORAN, MBI 222323) Known associates of JOYNT, possibly of Cassetta
       James F. SHUTT Jr, MBI 112367
       Edward CALLAHAN, MBI 177380
       Richard J CANNATA, MBI 233615
       Robert McCARRON, MBI 54394 (?)
       William SLUSKONIS, MBI 603756 (?)
       Beverly FABRIANO, MBI 603757

Photo September 1962
FPC (Right middle reproduced)
U-6 W-I U-16 W-I U-15
U-7 U-8 U-11 W-M U-15
MSBI BULL 4-65, Supp 9-1-65

Murder unsolved

MASSACHUSETTS DEPARTMENT OF PUBLIC SAFETY   CONFIDENTIAL POLICE BULLETIN

MURDER VICTIM: Joseph Romeo MARTIN, alias Romeo J MARTIN, "Bull"
                MBI 87410, FBI 2585485, Boston Mass PD 126332 (1964)

GIST: Body of Martin was found in his 1963 red automobile convertible on Harris
      Street, Revere, Mass, about 3:00 AM, Friday, a 65. Shots were heard shortly
      before, police were called, and body found in front seat, engine and wipers of
      car still running. Five gun shot wounds in upper left quarter of chest between
      heart and shoulder.

INVESTIGATING DEPARTMENT: Revere Police Department and Mass. State Police.

DESCRIPTION: Born 11-23-23 in Peabody, Mass. Also gave 11-24-24.
      White male, 5'10", 215 lbs, blue eyes, brown hair, medium build, medium complexio
      Tattoos: Kewpie, heart and dagger or arrow, boy blowing trumpet, "Evelyn"
      Father: Arthur P; Mother: Eva (Boucher); Wife: Diane.
ADDRESSES: 17 Hasey St, Revere (at death); car registered to 216 Revere Beach Pkw,
      433 Hanover St, Boston (1964)   Chelsea
      19 Fleet St, Boston (1964)
      11 Wyola Place, Dorchester (1963)   87 Long Pond Drive, Dracut (1958)
      62 Greenwich St, Dorchester (1962)   8 Highland St, Roxbury (1948-49)
      100 Lawn St, Roxbury (sometimes spelled Lorne) (1941-58)

OCCUPATIONS: Laborer, baker, lifeguard, gas attendant

ASSOCIATES: Wilfred J NICHOLAS, MBI 251047   Robert CARDILLO, MBI 130793 (?)
      Joseph BARBOZA Jr, alias BARRON, MBI 128227 Nicholas VENTOLA, MBI 115643
      Ronald CASSESSO, MBI 220277   Henry TAMELEO, Prov RI, MBI 10277
      Wilfred Roy FRENCH, MBI 284199   Ida WADE, MBI 240644
      Alexander CELESTE, MBI 118039   Andrew PAPPAS, MBI 133450
      Richard CASTUCCI, MBI 147401   Joseph SALVATI, MBI 162651
      Robert A DONATI, MBI 219208   Edward M GLYNN, MBI 128509
      Dorothy SASSO, MBI 297339   Peter PLAGENZA, MBI 135409
      Richard A DONATI, MBI 202962   Frank IMBRUGLIA, MBI 252818
      James "Vinnie" FLEMMI, MBI 140628   Fred CHIAMPA, MBI 117119 (?)
      Stephen FLEMMI, MBI 195188   James M MARTORANO, MBI 601655
      Edward "Wimpy" BENNETT, MBI 63445   Ralph LaMATTINA, MBI 83392
      Joseph ANSELMO, MBI 36971   Joseph COPPOLO, MBI 122250
      Raymond L S PATRIARCA, MBI 30408   Edward "Teddy" DEEGAN, MBI 129796
                                                                    (Murdered)

CRIMINAL RECORD: 1942 Refty, Brk Entering & Larc (14 counts); 1949 Army deserter;
      1951 State Prison, Brks, Larc Auto & Revolver in Vehicle; 1950 State Prison in
      Walla Walla, Wash, Rape; Attempted Escape & Escape, apprehended and returned;
      1958 MCI Walpole, Brk & Ent; 1964 PD Newton, Brk & Ent, for Grand Jury and out
      on bail; known gambler. Known to frequent the "Ebb-Tide", Revere, and lounges
      in Stuart St area, Boston.

Photo Oct. 1964
FPC (Rt thumb reproduced)
W-O W-I U-17 W-M W-I
W-I U-18 U-20 U-19 W-I
MSBI BULL 4-65, Supp 9-1-65

Murdered by Joe Barboza

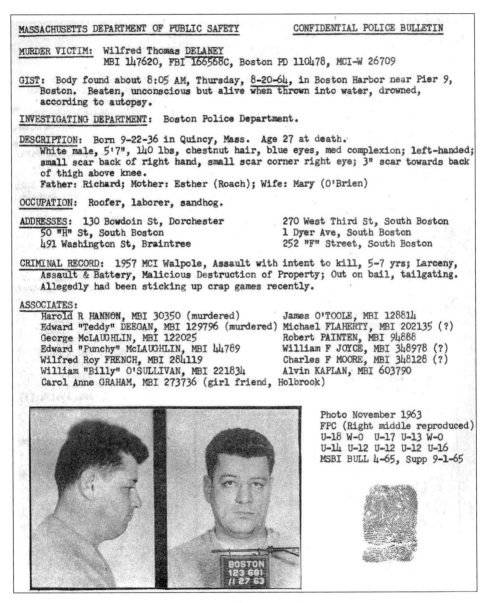

MASSACHUSETTS DEPARTMENT OF PUBLIC SAFETY   CONFIDENTIAL POLICE BULLETIN

MURDER VICTIM: Wilfred Thomas DELANEY
          MBI 147620, FBI 166568C, Boston PD 110478, MCI-W 26709

GIST: Body found about 8:05 AM, Thursday, 8-20-64, in Boston Harbor near Pier 9,
   Boston. Beaten, unconscious but alive when thrown into water, drowned,
   according to autopsy.

INVESTIGATING DEPARTMENT: Boston Police Department.

DESCRIPTION: Born 9-22-36 in Quincy, Mass. Age 27 at death.
   White male, 5'7", 140 lbs, chestnut hair, blue eyes, med complexion; left-handed;
   small scar back of right hand, small scar corner right eye; 3" scar towards back
   of thigh above knee.
   Father: Richard; Mother: Esther (Roach); Wife: Mary (O'Brien)

OCCUPATION: Roofer, laborer, sandhog.

ADDRESSES: 130 Bowdoin St, Dorchester   270 West Third St, South Boston
   50 "H" St, South Boston   1 Dyer Ave, South Boston
   491 Washington St, Braintree   252 "F" Street, South Boston

CRIMINAL RECORD: 1957 MCI Walpole, Assault with intent to kill, 5-7 yrs; Larceny,
   Assault & Battery, Malicious Destruction of Property; Out on bail, tailgating.
   Allegedly had been sticking up crap games recently.

ASSOCIATES:
   Harold R HANNON, MBI 30350 (murdered)   James O'TOOLE, MBI 128814
   Edward "Teddy" DEEGAN, MBI 129796 (murdered) Michael FLAHERTY, MBI 202135 (?)
   George McLAUGHLIN, MBI 122025   Robert PAINTEN, MBI 94888
   Edward "Punchy" McLAUGHLIN, MBI 44789   William F JOYCE, MBI 348978 (?)
   Wilfred Roy FRENCH, MBI 284119   Charles F MOORE, MBI 348128 (?)
   William "Billy" O'SULLIVAN, MBI 221834   Alvin KAPLAN, MBI 603790
   Carol Anne GRAHAM, MBI 273736 (girl friend, Holbrook)

Photo November 1963
FPC (Right middle reproduced)
U-18 W-0 U-17 U-13 W-0
U-14 U-12 U-12 U-12 U-16
MSBI BULL 4-65, Supp 9-1-65

Murdered by Winter Hill

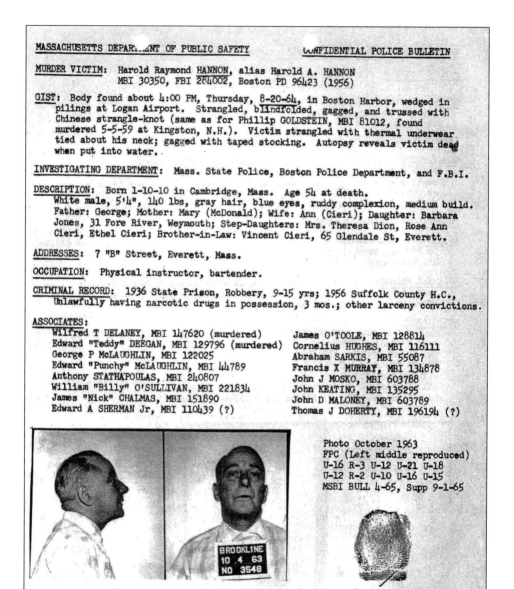

MASSACHUSETTS DEPAR...ENT OF PUBLIC SAFETY   CONFIDENTIAL POLICE BULLETIN

MURDER VICTIM: Harold Raymond HANNON, alias Harold A. HANNON
        MBI 30350, FBI 284002, Boston PD 96423 (1956)

GIST: Body found about 4:00 PM, Thursday, 8-20-64, in Boston Harbor, wedged in
    pilings at Logan Airport. Strangled, blindfolded, gagged, and trussed with
    Chinese strangle-knot (same as for Phillip GOLDSTEIN, MBI 81012, found
    murdered 5-5-59 at Kingston, N.H.). Victim strangled with thermal underwear
    tied about his neck; gagged with taped stocking. Autopsy reveals victim dead
    when put into water.

INVESTIGATING DEPARTMENT: Mass. State Police, Boston Police Department, and F.B.I.

DESCRIPTION: Born 1-10-10 in Cambridge, Mass. Age 54 at death.
    White male, 5'4", 140 lbs, gray hair, blue eyes, ruddy complexion, medium build.
    Father: George; Mother: Mary (McDonald); Wife: Ann (Cieri); Daughter: Barbara
    Jones, 31 Fore River, Weymouth; Step-Daughters: Mrs. Theresa Dion, Rose Ann
    Cieri, Ethel Cieri; Brother-in-Law: Vincent Cieri, 65 Glendale St, Everett.

ADDRESSES: 7 "B" Street, Everett, Mass.

OCCUPATION: Physical instructor, bartender.

CRIMINAL RECORD: 1936 State Prison, Robbery, 9-15 yrs; 1956 Suffolk County H.C.,
    Unlawfully having narcotic drugs in possession, 3 mos.; other larceny convictions.

ASSOCIATES:
Wilfred T DELANEY, MBI 147620 (murdered)	James O'TOOLE, MBI 128814
Edward "Teddy" DEEGAN, MBI 129796 (murdered)	Cornelius HUGHES, MBI 116111
George P McLAUGHLIN, MBI 122025	Abraham SARKIS, MBI 55087
Edward "Punchy" McLAUGHLIN, MBI 44789	Francis X MURRAY, MBI 134878
Anthony STATHAPOULAS, MBI 240807	John J MOSKO, MBI 603788
William "Billy" O'SULLIVAN, MBI 221834	John KEATING, MBI 135295
James "Nick" CHALMAS, MBI 151890	John D MALONEY, MBI 603789
Edward A SHERMAN Jr, MBI 110439 (?)	Thomas J DOHERTY, MBI 196194 (?)

Photo October 1963
FPC (Left middle reproduced)
U-16 R-3 U-12 U-21 U-18
U-12 R-2 U-10 U-16 U-15
MSBI BULL 4-65, Supp 9-1-65

BROOKLINE
10 4 63
NO 3548

Murdered by Winter Hill

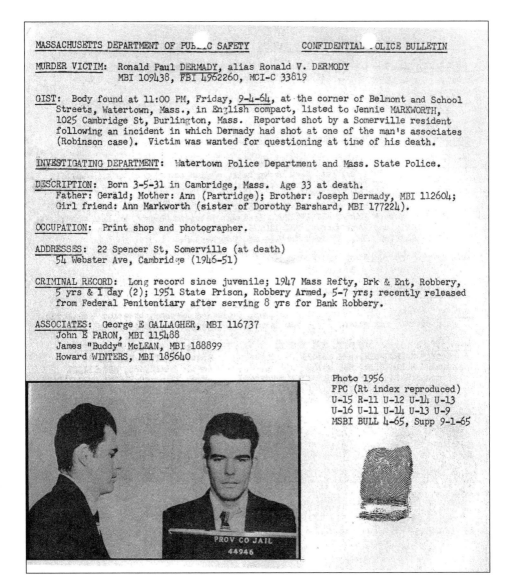

```
MASSACHUSETTS DEPARTMENT OF PUB__C SAFETY        CONFIDENTIAL _OLICE BULLETIN

MURDER VICTIM:  Ronald Paul DERMADY, alias Ronald V. DERMODY
                MBI 109438, FBI 4962260, MCI-C 33819

GIST:  Body found at 11:00 PM, Friday, 9-4-64, at the corner of Belmont and School
       Streets, Watertown, Mass., in English compact, listed to Jennie MARKWORTH,
       1025 Cambridge St, Burlington, Mass.  Reported shot by a Somerville resident
       following an incident in which Dermady had shot at one of the man's associates
       (Robinson case).  Victim was wanted for questioning at time of his death.

INVESTIGATING DEPARTMENT:  Watertown Police Department and Mass. State Police.

DESCRIPTION:  Born 3-5-31 in Cambridge, Mass.  Age 33 at death.
       Father: Gerald; Mother: Ann (Partridge); Brother: Joseph Dermady, MBI 112604;
       Girl friend: Ann Markworth (sister of Dorothy Barshard, MBI 177224).

OCCUPATION:  Print shop and photographer.

ADDRESSES:  22 Spencer St, Somerville (at death)
       54 Webster Ave, Cambridge (1946-51)

CRIMINAL RECORD:  Long record since juvenile; 1947 Mass Refty, Brk & Ent, Robbery,
       5 yrs & 1 day (2); 1951 State Prison, Robbery Armed, 5-7 yrs; recently released
       from Federal Penitentiary after serving 8 yrs for Bank Robbery.

ASSOCIATES:  George E GALLAGHER, MBI 116737
       John E PARON, MBI 115488
       James "Buddy" McLEAN, MBI 188899
       Howard WINTERS, MBI 185640
```

Photo 1956
FPC (Rt index reproduced)
U-15 R-11 U-12 U-14 U-13
U-16 U-11 U-14 U-13 U-9
MSBI BULL 4-65, Supp 9-1-65

PROV CO JAIL
44946

Murdered by Buddy McLean

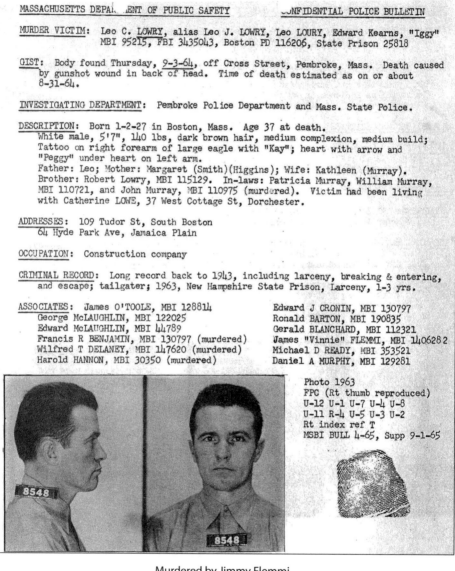

MASSACHUSETTS DEPAR.. .ENT OF PUBLIC SAFETY   .ONFIDENTIAL POLICE BULLETIN

MURDER VICTIM: Leo C. LOWRY, alias Leo J. LOWRY, Leo LOURY, Edward Kearns, "Iggy"
              MBI 95215, FBI 3435043, Boston PD 116206, State Prison 25818

GIST: Body found Thursday, 9-3-64, off Cross Street, Pembroke, Mass. Death caused
      by gunshot wound in back of head. Time of death estimated as on or about
      8-31-64.

INVESTIGATING DEPARTMENT: Pembroke Police Department and Mass. State Police.

DESCRIPTION: Born 1-2-27 in Boston, Mass. Age 37 at death.
      White male, 5'7", 140 lbs, dark brown hair, medium complexion, medium build;
      Tattoo on right forearm of large eagle with "Kay"; heart with arrow and
      "Peggy" under heart on left arm.
      Father: Leo; Mother: Margaret (Smith)(Higgins); Wife: Kathleen (Murray).
      Brother: Robert Lowry, MBI 115129. In-laws: Patricia Murray, William Murray,
      MBI 110721, and John Murray, MBI 110975 (murdered). Victim had been living
      with Catherine LOWE, 37 West Cottage St, Dorchester.

ADDRESSES: 109 Tudor St, South Boston
           64 Hyde Park Ave, Jamaica Plain

OCCUPATION: Construction company

CRIMINAL RECORD: Long record back to 1943, including larceny, breaking & entering,
      and escape; tailgater; 1963, New Hampshire State Prison, Larceny, 1-3 yrs.

ASSOCIATES: James O'TOOLE, MBI 128814   Edward J CRONIN, MBI 130797
      George McLAUGHLIN, MBI 122025   Ronald BARTON, MBI 190835
      Edward McLAUGHLIN, MBI 44789   Gerald BLANCHARD, MBI 112321
      Francis R BENJAMIN, MBI 130797 (murdered) James "Vinnie" FLEMMI, MBI 1406282
      Wilfred T DELANEY, MBI 147620 (murdered)   Michael D READY, MBI 353521
      Harold HANNON, MBI 30350 (murdered)   Daniel A MURPHY, MBI 129281

Photo 1963
FPC (Rt thumb reproduced)
U-12 U-1 U-7 U-4 U-8
U-11 R-4 U-5 U-3 U-2
Rt index ref T
MSBI BULL 4-65, Supp 9-1-65

8548

8548

Murdered by Jimmy Flemmi

```
MASSACHUSETTS DEPARTMENT OF PUBLIC SAFETY          CONFIDENTIAL POLICE INFORMATION

MURDER VICTIM:  Anthony D. SACRAMONE, MBI 292697

LIST:  Body found on Russell Street in Everett in his own car, 12 Noon, Saturday 10-17-64.
       Death caused by two bullets fired into back of head; also stabbed four times about the
       head and neck.

INVESTIGATING DEPARTMENT:  Everett Police Department and Mass. State Police

DESCRIPTION:  Born 8-13-42, East Boston, Mass.  Age 22 at death.
       White male, 5'5", 150 lbs., med. complexion
       Father: Daniel (Donato); Mother: Angelina & Josephine (Saldi); Brother: Albert J.,
       131 Whitford St., Roslindale

ADDRESSES:  47 Coolidge Street, Everett, Mass.

OCCUPATION:  Painter

CRIMINAL RECORD:  7-11-63 Traffic violation, Malden
                  (Under investigation for sale of harmful drugs at time of homocide)

ASSOCIATES:  William MARTIN, MBI 113542          Anthony STATHOPOULAS, MBI 160297
             Harold HANNON, MBI 30350 (Murdered) Robert DONATI, MBI 219208
             Richard DONATI, MBI 202962          Robert A. ARINELLA, MBI 289208
             Edward "Teddy" DEEGAN, MBI 129796
             (Murdered)

ADDED INFORMATION:  Frequented Ebb-Tide, Revere Beach.

                                          No Photographs or Fingerprints
                                                   Available
                                          MSBI BULL 4-65, Supp 9-1-65
```

Murdered by Teddy Deegan

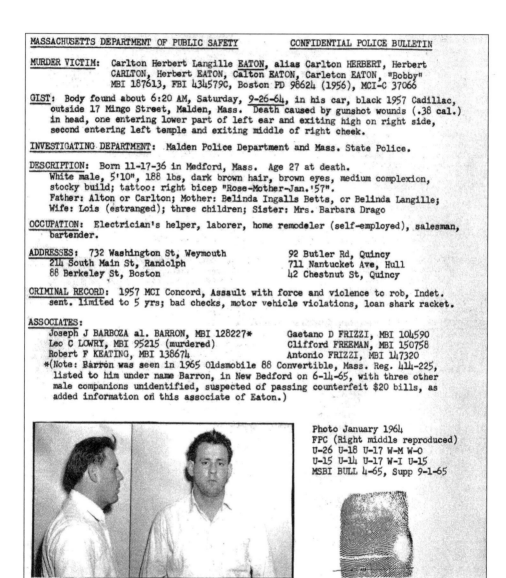

MASSACHUSETTS DEPARTMENT OF PUBLIC SAFETY   CONFIDENTIAL POLICE BULLETIN

MURDER VICTIM: Carlton Herbert Langille EATON, alias Carlton HERBERT, Herbert
                CARLTON, Herbert EATON, Calton EATON, Carleton EATON, "Bobby"
                MBI 187613, FBI 434579C, Boston PD 98624 (1956), MCI-C 37066

GIST: Body found about 6:20 AM, Saturday, 9-26-64, in his car, black 1957 Cadillac,
       outside 17 Mingo Street, Malden, Mass. Death caused by gunshot wounds (.38 cal.)
       in head, one entering lower part of left ear and exiting high on right side,
       second entering left temple and exiting middle of right cheek.

INVESTIGATING DEPARTMENT: Malden Police Department and Mass. State Police.

DESCRIPTION: Born 11-17-36 in Medford, Mass. Age 27 at death.
       White male, 5'10", 188 lbs, dark brown hair, brown eyes, medium complexion,
       stocky build; tattoo: right bicep "Rose-Mother-Jan.'57".
       Father: Alton or Carlton; Mother: Belinda Ingalls Betts, or Belinda Langille;
       Wife: Lois (estranged); three children; Sister: Mrs. Barbara Drago

OCCUPATION: Electrician's helper, laborer, home remodeler (self-employed), salesman,
       bartender.

ADDRESSES: 732 Washington St, Weymouth   92 Butler Rd, Quincy
            214 South Main St, Randolph   711 Nantucket Ave, Hull
            88 Berkeley St, Boston   42 Chestnut St, Quincy

CRIMINAL RECORD: 1957 MCI Concord, Assault with force and violence to rob, Indet.
       sent. limited to 5 yrs; bad checks, motor vehicle violations, loan shark racket.

ASSOCIATES:
    Joseph J BARBOZA al. BARRON, MBI 128227*   Gaetano D FRIZZI, MBI 104590
    Leo C LOWRY, MBI 95215 (murdered)   Clifford FREEMAN, MBI 150758
    Robert F KEATING, MBI 138674   Antonio FRIZZI, MBI 147320
    *(Note: Barron was seen in 1965 Oldsmobile 88 Convertible, Mass. Reg. 414-225,
    listed to him under name Barron, in New Bedford on 6-14-65, with three other
    male companions unidentified, suspected of passing counterfeit $20 bills, as
    added information on this associate of Eaton.)

                                    Photo January 1964
                                    FPC (Right middle reproduced)
                                    U-26 U-18 U-17 W-M W-O
                                    U-15 U-14 U-17 W-I U-15
                                    MSBI BULL 4-65, Supp 9-1-65

Murdered by Joe Barboza

MASSACHUSETTS DEPARTMENT OF PUBLIC SAFETY   CONFIDENTIAL POLICE INFORMATION

MURDER VICTIM: Edward P. HUBER, alias Edward Peter HUBER
          MBI 172500, FBI 225942C, Boston PD 121123 (1963)

GIST: Body found on Tuesday, 11-24-64, in Towers Brook, off Main Street, Hingham,
    Mass. Shot twice in the back.

INVESTIGATING DEPARTMENT: Hingham Police Department and Mass. State Police

DESCRIPTION: Born 10-7-19 in Boston, Mass. Age 45 at death.
    Father: Hiram; Mother; Bertha (Debolle); Wives: Marie (Cenga) and Ruth (Frazer);
    two children

OCCUPATION: Salesman

ADDRESSES: 658 Mass. Ave., Boston (1963)
    21 Mass. Ave., Boston (1964-65)
    88 Gainsboro St., Boston (1961)
    36 Myrtle St., Boston (1956)

CRIMINAL RECORD: Breaking & Entering in Boston and Watertown; 1956 Keene, N.H.,
    Malicious destruction of property

ASSOCIATES: William J TREANNIE, MBI 205938 (murdered); involved in narcotics with
    Robert E COOK, MBI 104565   victim.
    William MURRAY, MBI 134878
    Edward GOSS, MBI 127556
    Joseph AYUBE, MBI 302451

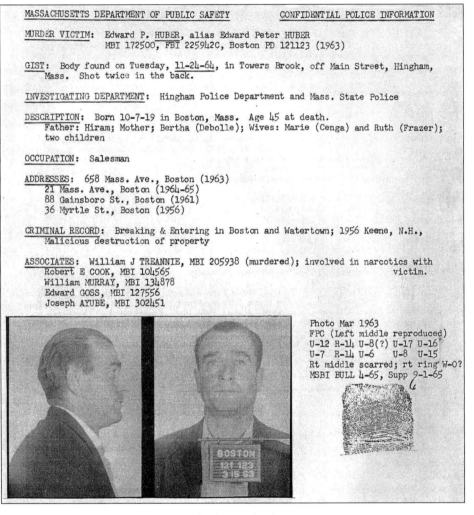

Photo Mar 1963
FPC (Left middle reproduced)
U-12 R-14 U-8(?) U-17 U-16
U-7 R-14 U-6   U-8 U-15
Rt middle scarred; rt ring W-0?
MSBI BULL 4-65, Supp 9-1-65

Murder unsolved

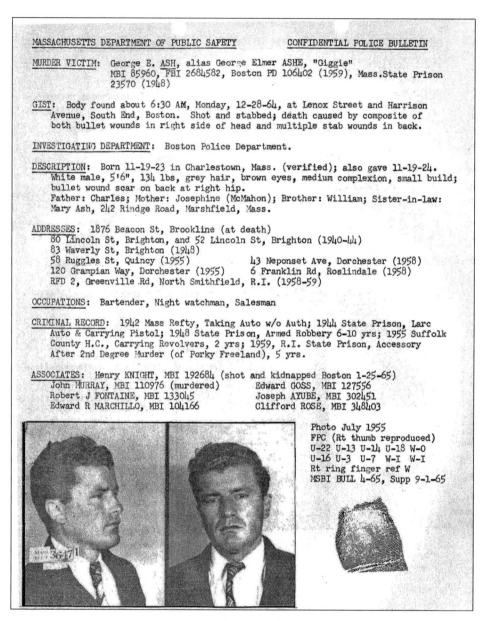

MASSACHUSETTS DEPARTMENT OF PUBLIC SAFETY   CONFIDENTIAL POLICE BULLETIN

MURDER VICTIM: George E. ASH, alias George Elmer ASHE, "Giggie"
        MBI 85960, FBI 2684582, Boston PD 106402 (1959), Mass.State Prison
        23570 (1948)

GIST: Body found about 6:30 AM, Monday, 12-28-64, at Lenox Street and Harrison
      Avenue, South End, Boston. Shot and stabbed; death caused by composite of
      both bullet wounds in right side of head and multiple stab wounds in back.

INVESTIGATING DEPARTMENT: Boston Police Department.

DESCRIPTION: Born 11-19-23 in Charlestown, Mass. (verified); also gave 11-19-24.
      White male, 5'6", 134 lbs, grey hair, brown eyes, medium complexion, small build;
      bullet wound scar on back at right hip.
      Father: Charles; Mother: Josephine (McMahon); Brother: William; Sister-in-law:
      Mary Ash, 242 Rindge Road, Marshfield, Mass.

ADDRESSES: 1876 Beacon St, Brookline (at death)
      80 Lincoln St, Brighton, and 52 Lincoln St, Brighton (1940-44)
      83 Waverly St, Brighton (1948)
      58 Ruggles St, Quincy (1955)   43 Neponset Ave, Dorchester (1958)
      120 Grampian Way, Dorchester (1955) 6 Franklin Rd, Roslindale (1958)
      RFD 2, Greenville Rd, North Smithfield, R.I. (1958-59)

OCCUPATIONS: Bartender, Night watchman, Salesman

CRIMINAL RECORD: 1942 Mass Refty, Taking Auto w/o Auth; 1944 State Prison, Larc
      Auto & Carrying Pistol; 1948 State Prison, Armed Robbery 6-10 yrs; 1955 Suffolk
      County H.C., Carrying Revolvers, 2 yrs; 1959, R.I. State Prison, Accessory
      After 2nd Degree Murder (of Porky Freeland), 5 yrs.

ASSOCIATES: Henry KNIGHT, MBI 192684 (shot and kidnapped Boston 1-25-65)
      John MURRAY, MBI 110976 (murdered)   Edward GOSS, MBI 127556
      Robert J FONTAINE, MBI 133045   Joseph AYUBE, MBI 302451
      Edward R MARCHILLO, MBI 104166   Clifford ROSE, MBI 348403

Photo July 1955
FPC (Rt thumb reproduced)
U-22 U-13 U-14 U-18 W-0
U-16 U-3 U-7 W-I W-I
Rt ring finger ref W
MSBI BULL 4-65, Supp 9-1-65

MANS
BUS 36471

Murdered by Jimmy Flemmi

The Doghouse

It was 1983, a late-summer weeknight in Boston. Boston LCN boss Gennaro "Jerry" Angiulo was having dinner at Francesca's on North Washington Street with two of his brothers, Frank and Mike. It was a short walk from their headquarters at 98 Prince Street, the Doghouse, as it was called from the days when their mother had sold hot dogs out of her little store there.

Her funeral entourage had had a Boston police escort when she'd died in 1976. That was the kind of clout Jerry Angiulo—"Jay," as he was known in the North End—wielded in those days.

In January 1981, the FBI had placed bugs in the Doghouse and in

"The Doghouse": 98 Prince Street

the social club run by his caporegime, Larry Baione, at 51 North Margin Street. More than a year later, the feds had formally informed the Angiulos, Baione and more than 60 other mobsters that their conversations had been recorded. But no one knew when the arrests would come, and the Angiulos were just going about their usual business—gambling and loansharking, mostly, but also grabbing whatever other opportunities came their way.

Suddenly the Angiulo table was surrounded. Towering above the slight 5-7, 66-year-old mobster was FBI agent, Ed Quinn, the man who Jerry had described as "the dirtiest Irish cop motherfucker in the entire world." As opposed to federal judge A. David Mazzone, whom Angiulo called "the dirtiest Italian motherfucker in the entire world."

QUINN WALKED toward Angiulo, who looked up from his pork chops. He instantly recognized his archnemesis.

"Mr. Quinn," he said.

"Mr. Angiulo. FBI. You're under arrest. Stand up."

He pulled Angiulo out of his seat and handcuffed his hands behind his back.

The Angiulo brothers at grand jury: Jerry is second from right.

"There's no reason for that," Angiulo said.

"That's the rules," Quinn said, "and this is how you go."

Shaking his head in disgust, Angiulo was led out of the restaurant, along with his two brothers. Over his shoulder, he yelled out one final statement of defiance, "I'll be back before my pork chops are cold."

It was September 19, 1983. Jerry Angiulo would not be released from prison until Sept. 10, 2007.

At the time, it was the biggest news in Boston. The FBI had brought down the Mafia. When the Angiulos went to the trial a year later, the courtroom was packed, and the story was covered day after day by newspapers from around the country. The tapes were played endlessly. Tourists had their photographs taken standing outside 98 Prince Street, cupping their ears as if they were listening in.

Angiulo himself provided a daily show in the courtroom. Whenever the author of this book wrote a column about the case, Angiulo would seek out my fellow *Herald* reporters and scream at them, "Tell Carr to lay off the Irish milk," or "You tell Howie I want to see him when he sobers up."

One morning, during a recess, he suddenly broke into song. To the tune of "Just a Gigolo," he belted out:

"I'm just a racketeer/That's all I ever hear/People know the game I'm

Boston LCN boss
Gennaro "Jerry" Angiulo

Jerry Angiulo at the burial of one
of his brothers

Surveillance photo of Stevie and Whitey

playing/When they lay me down to rest/With a lily on my chest/The gang will go on without me."

And so it did, but in a much reduced fashion, after his conviction in 1986 on racketeering, loansharking and gambling charges. The feds next bugged a bakery run in the Prudential Center by his successors, and then a actual Mafia initiation in Medford in 1989. His one-time hitmen, Whitey Bulger and Stevie Flemmi, emerged from the rubble of these ruinous federal investigations as the kingpins of organized crime in Boston.

As the years went by, the Doghouse bugging began to lose its luster, as it became clear just how corrupt the Boston FBI office was, and how the entire operation was designed at least as much to clear the Boston organized-crime field for Bulger and Flemmi as to break up the Mafia's alleged reign of terror.

Whitey and Stevie had been used as informants on the warrants for the Doghouse wiretaps; that way, the information then turned up could not be used to prosecute them. But the real informant work was done by a Chelsea bookie, Samuel Berkowitz, who was pardoned in 1987 by then-President Ronald Reagan.

During the bugging, Stevie Flemmi would later testify, he and Whitey had six Boston FBI agents on their payroll. One of them was Nick Gianturco, who would later recall Zip Connolly coming to the van to "sit on" the bug in "tan slacks, Gucci loafers, velvet velour shirt open at the chest with enough gold showing to be the envy of most members of the Gambino Crime Family."

Gushing articles had been writing about the hero special agents, books even. As the years went by, the outpouring of puffery seemed more and more inappropriate. This was the same FBI that had kept Whitey and Stevie out of the Winter Hill race-fixing indictment, and would later inform them about a DEA bug in Whitey's car, and then later about the Mafia's secret initiation at Guild Street. And in return the G-men received hundreds of thousands of dollars in cash bribes from their gangland paymasters.

Jeremiah O'Sullivan, federal prosecutor: "You got me."

The prosecutor was Jeremiah V. O'Sullivan, who spent his career tidying up messes for both Bulger brothers—in 1989, he broomed the 75 State Street extortion investigation against the Senate president.

By 2002 he was claiming he'd never known Whitey was an informant until it was in the papers. But under oath, in front of a Congressional committee, O'Sullivan was confronted with a memo showing he'd known Bulger was a rat as early as 1977.

"You got me," said O'Sullivan, who died in 2009.

Despite the fact that they've been largely forgotten, the tapes made at the Doghouse revealed in unprecedented

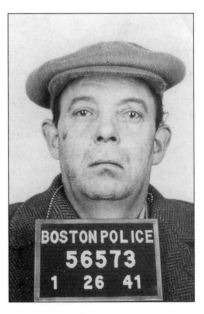

Old time mob boss Joe Lombardo

detail the inner workings of organized crime. They are also hilarious, not to mention over-the-top obscene. Angiulo, a genius bookie who had bought his way into the Mafia, was of course much more bloodthirsty than anyone who had "made their bones."

He'd come out of the U.S. Navy in 1945 at age 26, $12,000 cash in his pocket, early testimony to his uncommon skill as a gambler. Until the 1960's, he was not the "Jerry Angiulo" he would become on the tapes. He was only a bookmaker until 1950, when Sen. Estes Kefauver of Tennessee began his Senate hearings on organized crime. The aging hierarchy of the Boston LCN had no stomach for such a circus, and went into semi- or permanent retirement. There was a vacuum, and "Jay" Angiulo moved into it. He operated out of "Jay's Lounge" on Tremont Street. He cut his bookies in on the play—profit-sharing, you might say—and his business grew exponentially. He was soon the richest gangster in Boston, eclipsing Wimpy Bennett of Roxbury. He became the target for shakedowns, until he appeared in Federal Hill in Providence one day in the 1950s with a bag containing $50,000 cash for Raymond L.S. Patriarca, "the Man," the boss of the New England Mafia. Jerry bought his way into LCN, and one of his tormentors,

Providence boss
"Baby Shanks" Manocchio

Caporegime Peter Limone

Larry Baione: 1953

Rocco DiSeglio: note the pinky ring

Ilario M.A. Zannino, aka Larry Baione, became his muscle.

In 1967, Jerry was indicted on charges of authorizing a hit on Rocco DiSeglio (see "The Departed") who was part of a stickup crew robbing Mafia card and dice games. The main witness against Angiulo at trial was Mob hitman-turned-rat Joe Barboza. In January 1968 Angiulo beat the rap, and went outside the Pemberton Square courthouse and told reporters he was going home to his 73-year-old mother.

"Now I know what I was fighting for in World War II," said the former boatswain's mate.

From that moment on, he began playing the role of a big-time hoodlum. A few years later, he served a short stretch for assaulting a Coast Guardsman who gave him an order on his boat.

But if he wasn't yelling at you, Jerry Angiulo could be extremely funny, as he proved for three months in 1981 while the FBI was bugging the Doghouse, where he'd moved his headquarters after his mother's death in 1976.

For instance, here is Jerry, with his muscle, Larry Baione, on April 27, 1981. After Baione makes his usual first request—"Give me a drink," he says—he and Angiulo begin discussing the Racketeer-Influenced Corrupt Organizations (RICO) Act.

> ANGIULO: "I wouldn't be in a legitimate business for all the fuckin' money in the world to begin with. . . Our argument is, we're illegitimate business."
>
> BAIONE: "We're a shylock."
>
> ANGIULO: "We're a shylock."
>
> BAIONE: "Yeah."
>
> ANGIULO: "We're a fucking bookmaker."
>
> BAIONE: "Bookmaker."
>
> ANGIULO: "We're selling marijuana."
>
> BAIONE: "We're not infiltrating."
>
> ANGIULO: "We're, we're illegal here, illegal there, arsonists! We're every fucking thing."
>
> BAIONE: "Pimps!"
>
> ANGIULO: "So what?"
>
> BAIONE: "Prostitutes!"

On the wall of his office, Angiulo had one of those plaster-of-Paris plaques inscribed with a poem, "The Boss," cornball stuff about the responsibilities and duties of leadership. But Angiulo believed in his own twisted credo.

"When a man assumes leadership," he told Baione one day, "he forfeits the right to mercy. That's exactly what this fuckin' thing is all about. Exactly what it's all about."

In their world, a man never turned the other cheek, a man never endured an insult.

> BAIONE: "Why is it when, when Howie Ruben says to Johnny (Cincotti), Johnny, you suckin' cunt tonight, today?'"
>
> ANGIULO: "Even if he did suck it, you hit him!"

BAIONE: "I said, 'Johnny, call Howie Ruben in, this is an order. Ask him, 'Who the fuck is he think he is talking about suckin' cunt and bat him in the fuckin' mouth.'"

Ralphie "Chong" Lamattina explained what happened next: "I saw a guy fly out the room."

Here are a few of Angiulo's pensées on the events of the day:

Regarding the then-new casinos in Atlantic City: "You go to the same joint Atlantic City. They give you a fuckin' suite, they, they wine you, they dine you, they put oil up your ass. . ."

A guy his brother Frankie the Cad saw hanging out on the corner: "He was huh? High class motherfucker, this kid."

Why his numbers runners were always willing to take 18 months for contempt of the grand jury rather than testify: "We gave 'em the 300 a week when all they used to get was $90 to go and pick up one envelope. And you know, most of them came out and they were all fucking rich."

Will drug addicts stand up: "I'll fuckin' wager you anybody that deals in junk will tell the fuckin' motherfuckin' fed any fuckin' thing he wants."

Boston lawyer Martin Weinberg: "Marty what's his name that motherfucker Jew cocksucker?"

What happens to junkies who refuse to testify before a grand jury: "The problem is this kid goes to the can he ain't got no pills, no marijuana, he ain't got nothing. He starts to get them heebie-jeebies."

The division of territories in the Winter Hill Gang after the race-fixing indictments: "Whitey's got the whole of Southie. Stevie is got the whole of the South End. Johnny's got niggers. Howie knows this."

On the use of specialists: "I am sending for Vinny and his partner, Fat Vinny."

How easily a grand-jury indictment against him could be written: "There's no fiction here. They don't have to fictionize."

JERRY ANGIULO liked to tell his men how to kill. He'd had to buy his own protection, but now he was an expert on mayhem. On March 19, 1981, he brought soldier Richie Gambale into his office and asked him about a guy Jerry suspected was going to talk to the grand jury that had already called Jerry's son Jason, as well as Skinny Kazonis.

"Strangle him," Jerry said. "And get rid of him. Hit him in the fucking head."

Apparently, though, Richie has neglected the simplest of preparations for a hit. Jerry explodes.

"You don't have. . . You ain't got a hot car. You ain't got nothin'. You think I need tough guys. I need intelligent tough guys."

Jerry then tries to explain to Richie that this guy has more on him than on anyone else in the crew. Which puts Richie in extreme peril.

"Richie, you want to be careful because you can be killed. Because the only guy he's gonna bury is you." Suddenly, for once Jerry is overcome with remorse, and regret for the life he chose, as Michael Corleone put it.

"The fuckin' life, it stinks. I don't need that fuckin' shit. Okay, buddy? You get him where you want him, don't ever tell me that something happened and we had to pass, because you will be in more fuckin' trouble than you were to start with. You understand? Even if you gotta snatch him off the fuckin' street. You understand that?"

Now, more specific instructions:

"Get out of the car and you stomp him. Bing! You hit him in the fuckin' head and leave him right in the fuckin' spot. Do you understand?"

Next, Jerry discusses how to set it up.

"Tell me what your plan is tonight. I want to hear it. Did he say to you, call me at the house?"

"I don't know," Gambale says.

"You used to go to the fuckin motherfuckin' Mousetrap to get your fuckin' money. See if he's in the Mousetrap. Give him a phone call. 'Where are

Sammy Granito: convicted
with the Angiulos

ya going? I'll meet ya." . . . Hey kid, don't call him at 10 o'clock and you ain't gonna meet him until 5 in the morning, 'cause he'll tell 20 fuckin' people he gotta meet Richie.

"Meet him tonight. I hope it happens tonight. That's why I'm sendin' you because I know you gotta supposedly call him. Understand?"

The fact that Richie hasn't stolen a car continues to bother Jerry.

"You ain't got a hot car. Just hit him in the fuckin' head and stab him, okay? The jeopardy is just a little too much for me. You understand American?"

The hit never took place.

IN THE pre-cocaine Boston underworld, the Angiulos' gambling and loansharking rackets were fabulously lucrative. According to an FBI affidavit at their trial, during 1982 alone, the Angiulos purchased more than $1,765,000 in cashiers' checks from the Bank of Boston.

Of that money, the feds wrote, "over $250,000 was purchased with 'new cash,' i.e., cash that was not withdrawn from any existing accounts."

More than $270,000 of that money went to a white-shoe investment company, Cowen & Co. They purchased another $250,000 in cashiers' check from the Provident Bank, which also went to Cowen & Co.

In raids on 95 and 98 Prince Street in 1981, FBI agents seized $383,000 in cash. Frankie the Cad Angiulo had $7000 on his person, $40,000 in a dresser drawer at 95 Prince Street, and $300,000 in "notes drawn on the Chrysler Financial Corporation" in a safe at 98 Prince Street.

In 1980 Jerry purchased a 68-foot yacht in Palm Beach and modestly named it the "St. Gennaro." The purchase price was $300,000—bought "with consecutively numbered cashiers' checks on the First National Bank of Boston."

Carmen Tortora

When he died in 2009, his son Gennaro, the owner of G&J Towing in Revere, said that buying that yacht had been the proudest moment of his father's life.

Danny Angiulo

IN FEBRUARY 1981 one of Larry Baione's guys, Carmen Tortora, had a big problem. He was coming up for a sentencing the next day in federal court on loansharking charges. He'd left a death threat on a telephone-answering machine.

In the late afternoon, Larry brought him up to the Doghouse to say goodbye to the Angiulo brothers. But Nicky had already gone home, and Jerry wasn't around. Only Frankie the Cad, who lived across the street, was still around.

Carmen stuck his hand out. "Nice meetin' ya."

"Nice meetin' ya?" Frankie said in surprise. "Where you goin'? I ain't goin' nowhere. You going away for a little while. You'll be back. What's this 'Nice meeting you?'"

Donny and Mikey Angiulo arrive with Skinny Kazonis, and Larry explains to them the sad story of why Carmen is going away, because of a rat.

Mikey Angiulo

"This is an asshole he knows from the corner. He had himself wired up for $200."

Mikey does the right thing. He asks the defendant whether he wants red or white wine.

"Red," says Carmen.

"You don't know the fuckin' difference," Larry sneers. After the drinks are poured, Danny Angiulo offers a toast.

"Carmen," he says, "to your health. . .and a very short stay."

Larry interrupts: "Give me a fuckin' double martini."

Mikey Angiulo: "Any idea where you're going, though?"

"Lewisburg."

After finishing their drinks, Larry and Carmen head back to 51 North Margin Street. Larry gives him his instructions for the next day's sentencing.

"Call me. Call me from the court. Will you please?"

"My wife or me will call you," Carmen says.

"All right. I hope it's you kid." In other words, he hopes Carmen isn't immediately taken into custody to begin his sentence. "I hope I hear your voice tomorrow, pal."

Carmen's a little down. "I'm gonna have five or six more martinis."

"No," Larry says, "go home."

Carmen wearily trudges down the stairs, and Larry continues his conversation with an unknown male, telling him that everything depends on whether Carmen gets a consecutive or a concurrent sentence. If he gets two five-year concurrent sentences "he'll see the (parole) board in 18 months. That's what we're shooting for."

The unknown male asks Baione if Carmen can withdraw his guilty plea.

"Yeah," says Larry, "but he'll get 100 years if he goes to trial. Hasn't got a fuckin' chance. He's got a 14-page (transcript). 'I'll kill you, you cocksucker. Your family, I'll kill everybody you know. You pay the fuckin' vig, and you took 250, you owe 600. And I'll chop you in little pieces.' Forget about it. Why do you think I told him to cop out? Hey, that's part of the game, he's 33 years old, he's a big boy, he's got good shoulders, he'll go and do his fuckin' time."

Larry's planning on getting Carmen onto the prison farm, "a fuckin' joke." But he still can't understand why someone would go running to the feds over a lousy 250 bucks.

"You know," he says, "if it was 25,000 I could understand the guy panicking. He can't get it up. But 250 motherfuckin'. . . Cocksucker that you are. You know he went to the feds and they wired him and oh how he set him up. . .'Don't hurt my wife.'"

A couple of weeks later, Larry and Jerry are sitting in the Doghouse, and Larry brings up Carmen's name. It turns out, he didn't go to Lewisburg after all.

"Carmen's in New Hampshire state prison," Larry says. "And his wife called me yesterday and she said, 'Larry, Carmen's goin' out of his mind. Can't stand it.' I said, 'Listen Bonnie. That's the way it is.' 'No,' she says, 'you don't understand. He wants a TV in the worst way because he don't read. . .' I says, 'It'll be up there today,' I says. 'What do you think she said to me?'"

"Send a machine gun cake?" That was Jerry Angiulo, always the soothing thought for someone down on their luck.

JERRY WANTED his son Jason in the mob. But Jason just plain didn't have it in him. He was 23, and he much preferred hanging at the trendy nightspot, Jason's (not named after him) to the Doghouse. But Jerry insisted that he learn the business from the ground up, by running Las Vegas nights—gambling events for churches and other charities.

Skinny Kazonis: Greek associate

For Jerry, gaming was second nature. He'd been gambling his entire life. It was his business, and his hobby. For Jason, it was neither.

"This motherfucker don't know a fucking thing," he tells Jason one day, addressing his own son in the third person. "He don't know that fucking much about gambling. All he knows is you win or lose, and you walk around smoking cigarettes."

"Yeah?" says Jason. "Let me tell you—"

"You talk," says his father, "and I'll hit you with a fucking bottle. . .Why, you fuckin' idiot you!"

Tony Angiulo: sixth brother, died young

The problem at this most recent Las Vegas night was that Jason's dealers had continued using the same playing cards hour after hour, hand after hand. Jerry had instructed him, don't use the cards for very long, because you'll give a hustler a chance to mark them. But Jason has an excuse.

"There was only five decks of cards 'cause we ran out of fucking cards 'cause some asshole spilled fucking shit on the bar. Then we dropped them on the fucking floor. Somebody—"

"Who?" interrupts Jerry. "The asshole?"

"Some idiot playing at the fucking table."

"Think it could have been deliberate?"

Then they start talking about craps. Once again, Jerry is telling him, get rid of the dice after no more than 90 minutes. Jason tries to cut in but Jerry won't let him speak.

"Fucking, motherfucking, big mouth cocksucker, shut up!"

Jason: "You gonna listen to me?"

"No, you motherfucker. Now shut up." Jerry was yelling now. "Let me tell you something, huh? I've been in the crap business when you were, weren't born you cocksucker that you are. A pair of dice that's been used more than two hours, that set goes in your pocket and they're thrown down the fucking sewer. Do you understand that? That's a fucking order because you're a fucking idiot. Now just shut up."

And another thing, Jerry says, don't be telling anybody about the financial arrangements for these Las Vegas nights.

"What the fuck are you telling you got 50 percent coming? It's for charity, you fuckin' asshole."

As a federal grand jury began closing in on Jerry in early 1981, he was concerned about Jason's ability to stand up. He had no experience taking the heat. He'd never done time. He was, as Jerry derisively told him over and over again, "a college boy. . . a fucking college boy."

Jerry's ambition in his Boston English High Class of '36 yearbook had been to be a "criminal attorney," and he read voraciously on legal matters, especially the RICO statute. But he still tried to play the street guy, even with his own son.

One day, he preps Jason for his upcoming grand-jury appearance by asking what his business is, what he runs.

Jason replies, "Primarily the club."

"Prime who?" Jerry explodes. "Don't use them fucking words with me! They're too big! 'Primarily the club.' What club?"

Another time, Jerry is explaining to Jason and Skinny Kazonis about the ins and outs of what he calls an "892"—loansharking under the Extortionate Credit Act.

"An enterprise," he instructs his students. "Remember that word, enterprise. And it isn't the USS aircraft carrier either. Enterprise! See what you're doing here right now? You're making an enterprise. All it takes is one guy."

At another point, he theorizes about how Jason could save himself—by ratting out his father.

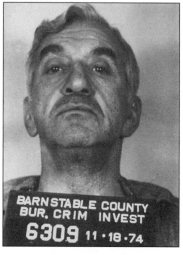

Gennaro Angiulo

"It's a hell of a fucking theory, ain't it? You wouldn't be the first son that turned in his father. Take my word on it. That I can bet you on. And on the other hand, you must remember there are a lot of guys in Leavenworth and a lot of guys in Lewisburg that protected their sons. They went, 'He had nothing to do with it, it was me.'"

Jerry paused to let Jason consider the odds of that happening with "Jay."

"There'll be no such fucking thing here!" Jerry screamed, answering his own question. "We will be men, or mice!"

In the end, Jason went away, just like his old man. His Bureau of Prisons number was 13667-038. He was finally released from prison in September 1989. He is now 57 years old.

Frankie "the Cad" Angiulo

Jerry Angiulo was 90 years old when he died in 2009. He was buried out of St. Leonard's Church in the North End on the 80th birthday of Whitey Bulger.

As a Navy veteran, he had an honor guard from the USS Constitution. The funeral procession was led by a flatbed trunk carrying more than 190 floral bouquets. Dozens of members of the Hells Angels motorcycle club showed up on Harleys, wearing their colors, to pay their respects.

The eulogy in front of his flag-draped casket was delivered by his younger son, Gennaro Jay Angiulo, Jr., age 38, the owner of G&J Towing in Revere. He recalled his father's "proudest day," when he launched his 68-foot yacht, the St. Gennaro, bought with those cashiers' checks from the First National Bank of Boston, which no longer existed.

"The government caught up to Dad and the boys," he said of his father and uncles, only one of whom, Frankie the Cad, survived. "And Dad was sent to a 20-year college with a full scholarship."

When he was finally freed, in 2007, Jerry Angiulo moved back to his oceanfront property in Nahant, spending time with his son, teaching him the meaning of respect, telling the younger man, "Don't abuse it, you can't buy it, you have to earn it."

Finally, just before the standing-room-only-crowd gave him a standing ovation, the younger Angiulo said:

"Celebrate his life. Because in the words of the great Frank Sinatra, Jerry did it his way."

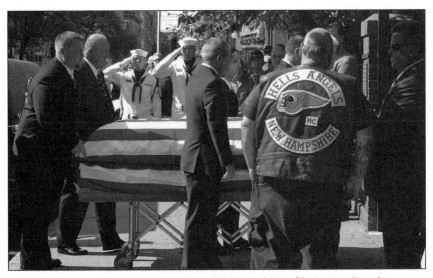

On September 3, 2009, Jerry Angiulo is buried out of St. Leonard's in the North End with Navy and Hells Angels honor guards. Ironically, the funeral took place on Whitey Bulger's 80th birthday.

FBI Most Wanted

It may not be the most effective crime-fighting tool ever devised, but for the FBI, the Most Wanted list certainly has no competition in terms of favorable publicity generated for the Bureau.

The Most Wanted list dates back to 1950, when a wire-service reporter inquired if the FBI had a list of most-wanted fugitives. The resulting story turned out to be a public-relations bonanza. Marketing genius that he was, Director J. Edgar Hoover soon made the "Ten Most Wanted Fugitives" list an official program. It debuted on March 14, 1950.

The list has endured much criticism over the years. The speed with which fugitives added to the list were apprehended—sometimes the same day—led cynics to believe that Hoover was holding off on some announcements until his agents had actually located the fugitive and had him staked out.

Later, around 1970, the FBI began adding student radicals, who often proved to be better at staying on the lam than Hoover's usual prey. The average time of apprehension—always a matter of pride for Hoover and his successors—began creeping upwards, and the FBI took to quietly dropping some student fugitives from the list a few years after they'd slipped from view, and the headlines.

One such person was Katherine Power, a Catholic school girl radicalized at Brandeis University in Waltham. She hooked up with fellow student Susan Saxe and stopped wearing a bra. She was a radical now. In the fall of 1970, with the assistance of three hardened Walpole ex-cons, the two coeds robbed a bank in Brighton and murdered a Boston patrolman, Walter Schroeder.

Both Saxe and Power were added to the Most Wanted list, and Saxe remained free until 1975. She cut a deal with prosecutors and only served seven years.

Susan Saxe

Katherine Ann Power wanted poster

As for Katherine Ann Power, in 1984, almost 14 years after vanishing, she was quietly dropped from the Most Wanted list. After years of living in Oregon as "Alice Louise Metzinger," Power turned herself in to Massachusetts authorities in 1993 and pleaded guilty to manslaughter. She was released in 1999 and is now 65 years old.

BOSTON HAS had its share of Most Wanted over the years, but some of the FBI posters are no longer available. However, probably the most famous

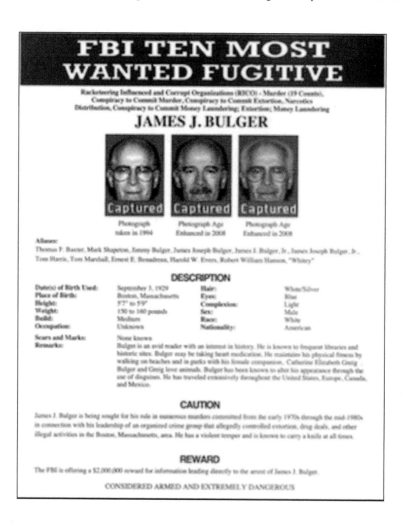

poster of all is still around, in the millions of copies, in multiple languages.

Eventually, the reward for Whitey was raised to $2 million.

The first Bostonians to make the list were two of the Brinks robbers, perpetrators of what was in 1950 the largest robbery in U.S. history—when seven men dressed as Brinks guards got into the armored-car terminal in the North End and made off with $1,218,211 in cash.

Carleton O'Brien

The plan was to lay low, but there were too many people involved. The first to demand more money was one James "Specs" O'Keefe. He wanted another $63,000 in cash. The remaining crew members immediately began looking for a hitman to get rid of O'Keefe. But before they could move, there was another twist in the story. An ex-con named Carleton O'Brien, a veteran Rhode Island mobster, as one of the masterminds of the job.

Three days later, on May 17, 1952, O'Brien was shot to death, either by Brinks plotters or by the Rhode Island Mafia, which had been muscling into O'Brien's rackets.

In 1954, Elmer "Trigger" Burke, from the Hells Kitchen neighborhood on the West Side of Manhattan that would later spawn the Westies, got the contract. In June of that year, Specs O'Keefe led the New York hitman on a wild chase through Dorchester, with Trigger wildly firing a machine gun at him, wounding O'Keefe before escaping a police dragnet.

Trigger was caught a few days later, but escaped for a year before being apprehended by the FBI in South Carolina. He was never tried in Boston, but was instead convicted and executed at Sing Sing in 1958 for the drunken murder of a West Side drinking buddy named Poochie.

Oddly, Trigger Burke never made the Most Wanted list, but below are a couple of his New York wanted posters.

Specs, meanwhile, was convicted on weapons charges in 1954, and after receiving a 27-month sentence, he spilled the beans on everybody.

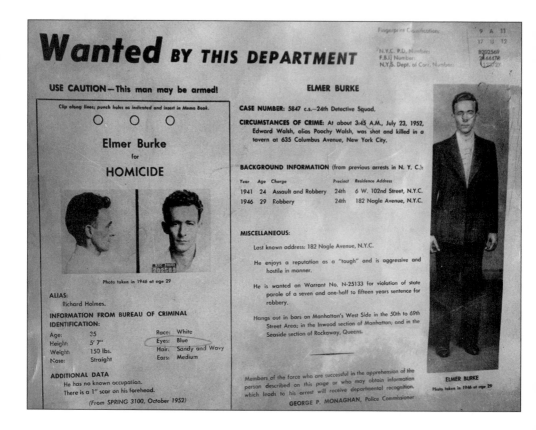

Wanted BY THIS DEPARTMENT

Fingerprint Classification: 9 A 11 17 U 12
N.Y.C. P.D. Number:
F.B.I. Number:
N.Y.S. Dept. of Corr. Number:

USE CAUTION—This man may be armed!

ELMER BURKE

Clip along lines; punch holes as indicated and insert in Memo Book.

Elmer Burke
for
HOMICIDE

Photo taken in 1946 at age 29

ALIAS:
Richard Holmes.

INFORMATION FROM BUREAU OF CRIMINAL IDENTIFICATION:

Age:	35	Race:	White
Height:	5' 7"	Eyes:	Blue
Weight:	150 lbs.	Hair:	Sandy and Wavy
Nose:	Straight	Ears:	Medium

ADDITIONAL DATA
He has no known occupation.
There is a 1" scar on his forehead.

(From SPRING 3100, October 1952)

CASE NUMBER: 5847 c.s.—24th Detective Squad.

CIRCUMSTANCES OF CRIME: At about 3:45 A.M., July 23, 1952, Edward Walsh, alias Poochy Walsh, was shot and killed in a tavern at 635 Columbus Avenue, New York City.

BACKGROUND INFORMATION (from previous arrests in N. Y. C.):

Year	Age	Charge	Precinct	Residence Address
1941	24	Assault and Robbery	24th	6 W. 102nd Street, N.Y.C.
1946	29	Robbery	24th	182 Nagle Avenue, N.Y.C.

MISCELLANEOUS:

Last known address: 182 Nagle Avenue, N.Y.C.

He enjoys a reputation as a "tough" and is aggressive and hostile in manner.

He is wanted on Warrant No. N-25133 for violation of state parole of a seven and one-half to fifteen years sentence for robbery.

Hangs out in bars on Manhattan's West Side in the 50th to 69th Street Area; in the Inwood section of Manhattan; and in the Seaside section of Rockaway, Queens.

Members of the force who are successful in the apprehension of the person described on this page or who may obtain information which leads to his arrest will receive departmental recognition.

GEORGE P. MONAGHAN, Police Commissioner

ELMER BURKE
Photo taken in 1946 at age 29

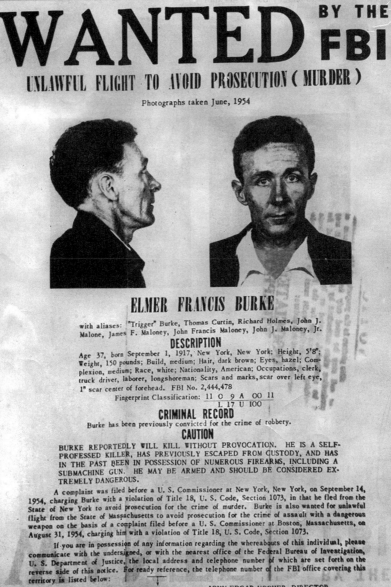

WANTED BY THE FBI

UNLAWFUL FLIGHT TO AVOID PROSECUTION (MURDER)

Photographs taken June, 1954

ELMER FRANCIS BURKE

with aliases: "Trigger" Burke, Thomas Curtin, Richard Holmes, John J. Malone, James F. Maloney, John Francis Maloney, John J. Maloney, Jr.

DESCRIPTION

Age 37, born September 1, 1917, New York, New York; Height, 5'8"; Weight, 150 pounds; Build, medium; Hair, dark brown; Eyes, hazel; Complexion, medium; Race, white; Nationality, American; Occupations, clerk, truck driver, laborer, longshoreman; Scars and marks, scar over left eye, 1" scar center of forehead. FBI No. 2,444,478

Fingerprint Classification: 11 O 9 A 00 11
L 17 U 100

CRIMINAL RECORD

Burke has been previously convicted for the crime of robbery.

CAUTION

BURKE REPORTEDLY WILL KILL WITHOUT PROVOCATION. HE IS A SELF-PROFESSED KILLER, HAS PREVIOUSLY ESCAPED FROM CUSTODY, AND HAS IN THE PAST BEEN IN POSSESSION OF NUMEROUS FIREARMS, INCLUDING A SUBMACHINE GUN. HE MAY BE ARMED AND SHOULD BE CONSIDERED EXTREMELY DANGEROUS.

A complaint was filed before a U. S. Commissioner at New York, New York, on September 14, 1954, charging Burke with a violation of Title 18, U. S. Code, Section 1073, in that he fled from the State of New York to avoid prosecution for the crime of murder. Burke is also wanted for unlawful flight from the State of Massachusetts to avoid prosecution for the crime of assault with a dangerous weapon on the basis of a complaint filed before a U. S. Commissioner at Boston, Massachusetts, on August 31, 1954, charging him with a violation of Title 18, U. S. Code, Section 1073.

If you are in possession of any information regarding the whereabouts of this individual, please communicate with the undersigned, or with the nearest office of the Federal Bureau of Investigation, U. S. Department of Justice, the local address and telephone number of which are set forth on the reverse side of this notice. For ready reference, the telephone number of the FBI office covering this territory is listed below:

JOHN EDGAR HOOVER, DIRECTOR
FEDERAL BUREAU OF INVESTIGATION
UNITED STATES DEPARTMENT OF JUSTICE
WASHINGTON 25, D. C.
TELEPHONE, NATIONAL 8-7117

Wanted Flyer No. 160
September 15, 1954

On January 12, 1956, with the statute of limitations about to run out, the FBI moved to round up the eight surviving suspects. They got six, but missed James Ignatius Faherty and Thomas Francis Richardson, both of whom were quickly added to the Most Wanted list.

Faherty and Richardson had been partners in crime since 1934. Faherty, incredibly, was working at a bank when the FBI came after him. On May 16, 1956, both fugitives were captured in an apartment in Dorchester. Faherty had been hidden by ex-con William Cameron, and there were rumors he had turned the pair in for the reward. Cameron was shot to death three weeks later.

James Faherty

GEORGE MCLAUGHLIN was the youngest of the fearsome McLaughlin brothers of Charlestown. In the early 1960's, the McLaughlins were embroiled in a ferocious gang war with the McLean mob of Somerville, which later became the Winter Hill Gang.

However, McLaughlin's career ended not because of mob violence, but because he senselessly murdered a 21-year-old bank clerk at a christening in Roxbury in March 1964. Two months later he was added to the Most Wanted list.

Stevie Flemmi, Whitey Bulger's future partner, was an informant for FBI agent H. Paul Rico. According to his confession, Flemmi was visited at his store in 1965 by Rico, who asked Stevie to procure a "throw down"— untraceable—gun for him.

Flemmi asked why, and Rico said that the FBI had located McLaughlin, whose brother Punchy had been recorded on an illegal "gypsy" wiretap calling Hoover and Rico "fags." Rico wanted to wipe out the McLaughlins (later that year he would direct Flemmi's murder of George's brother Punchy at a bus stop).

WANTED

BY THE FBI

UNLAWFUL FLIGHT TO AVOID PROSECUTION (ARMED ROBBERY

Photograph taken November 1941

THOMAS FRANCIS RICHARDSON

with aliases: James Gately, Thomas Kendricks, Patrick T. Nash, Thomas Richards, Thomas W. Richardson, "Sandy"

DESCRIPTION

Age 48, born March 22, 1907, Boston, Massachusetts (not verified); Height, 5'7" to 5'8½"; Weight, 140-145 pounds; Build, medium; Hair, gray; Eyes, blue; Complexion, ruddy; Race, white; Nationality, American; Occupation, longshoreman; Scars and marks, scar on left side of head; Remarks, may be wearing rimless eyeglasses, has a full upper and lower denture, has a noticeably hoarse voice, is a chain cigarette smoker, is fastidious in personal neatness, reported to be a heavy drinker of intoxicants and is reported to have a habit of losing false teeth when drinking. FBI No. 838,889

Fingerprint Classification: $\underline{15\ M\ 17\ W\ MIO\ 9}$
$M\ \ 3\ W\ OOO$

CRIMINAL RECORD

Richardson has been convicted for armed robbery.

CAUTION

RICHARDSON SHOULD BE CONSIDERED ARMED AND EXTREMELY DANGEROUS. EXERCISE ALL CAUTION IN ATTEMPTING TO APPREHEND.

A complaint was filed before a U. S. Commissioner at Boston, Massachusetts, on January 19, 1956, charging Richardson with a violation of Title 18, U. S. Code, Section 1073, in that he fled from the State of Massachusetts to avoid prosecution for the crime of armed robbery of Brink's Incorporated which occurred at Boston, Massachusetts, on January 17, 1950. This Wanted Flyer supersedes Wanted Flyer No. 182. Complaints filed January 11, 1956, at Boston, Massachusetts, charging Richardson with conspiracy to violate the Robbery and Theft of Government Property Statutes; violation of and conspiracy to violate the Federal Bank Robbery Statute were dismissed on January 19, 1956.

If you are in possession of any information regarding the whereabouts of this individual, please communicate with the undersigned, or with the nearest office of the Federal Bureau of Investigation, U. S. Department of Justice, the local address and telephone number of which are set forth on the reverse side of this notice. For ready reference, the telephone number of the FBI office covering this territory is listed below:

JOHN EDGAR HOOVER, DIRECTOR
FEDERAL BUREAU OF INVESTIGATION
UNITED STATES DEPARTMENT OF JUSTICE
WASHINGTON 25, D. C.
TELEPHONE, NATIONAL 8-7117

Wanted Flyer No. 182A
January 19, 1956

Rico said he had several agents who were planning to raid the apartment that night. Rico would be first in, and he would plant the gun, after which he and the other agents would murder McLaughlin and whoever else was there.

Flemmi obtained the gun and gave it to Rico. But the next morning the photos appeared on the front pages of the Boston newspapers.

In his confession, Flemmi said he later asked what had gone wrong, and Rico told him that he "wasn't sure" about one of the agents, so he'd been unable to kill McLaughlin. Now 87, McLaughlin remains imprisoned in Massachusetts. Flemmi never got his gun back.

George McLaughlin at age 37

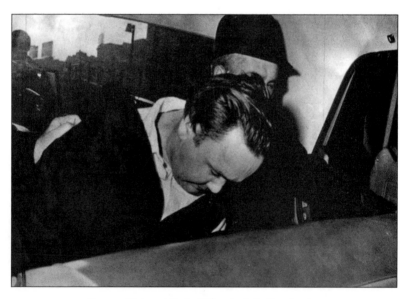

George McLaughlin in FBI custody in Dorchester

Once the Most Wanted fugitive was under arrest, the local police would be notified.

IN 1966, local Mafia mobsters lured two of imprisoned gangster Joe Barboza's gunsels to a North End night-club known as the Nite Lite. The two hoods had collected $78,000 cash for Barboza's $90,000 bail, and the LCN was supposed to provide the last $12,000.

Instead, they murdered the two gangsters, Tash Bratsos and Thomas DePrisco, and stole the money. The bodies were dumped in a Cadillac that was abandoned in South Boston to give the impression that Irish gangsters had committed the crime.

No one was fooled, and several arrests were quickly made.

A few months later, "In Town," as the local Mafia was then known, began

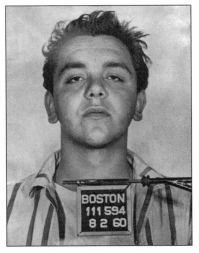

Carmen Gagliardi: seven years before running the red light

fretting about one of the men who'd been in the Nite Lite that evening. His name was Joe Lanzi. A contract was put out.

On the night of April 18, 1967, cops saw a car speeding through a red light in Medford. They gave chase, and when the car stopped, two men jumped out and took off in opposite directions. Inside the car was the body of Joe Lanzi, who had been shot just moments earlier.

One of the killers who escaped on foot that night was Carmen Gagliardi, a local plug ugly. He was added to the Most Wanted list in June 1967, and was captured hiding at his mother's house in December 1968. He eventually died of a drug overdose in prison in 1975.

This is the mugshot the FBI sent out when Gagliardi made the Most Wanted list—minus the city ID, of course.

Note that his 1965 mugshot is from the Malden police department; when the FBI released it, the Malden PD identification was gone. After all, J. Edgar Hoover couldn't have the FBI sharing credit with anyone.

JOE MCDONALD was a legendary criminal in Boston, a "man's man," according to hitman Johnny Martorano.

McDonald was a binge drinker, and as he got older, he got crazier, at least when he drank. In 1973, he tracked a fugitive member of Al Angeli's gang to Fort Lauderdale and walked into a trailer where the man, a former protégé of McDonald's, was holed up. McDonald jumped the hood, wrestled him to the ground and then shot him five times in the head.

In the 1970's, he and his partner Jimmy Sims were two of the founding members of the Winter Hill Gang, but they soon went on the lam.

It seems that they had been sticking up stamp and coin dealers, and one had decided to testify against them. Sims and McDonald tracked the potential witness to California, and saw him inside a house.

Impulsively, McDonald pulled a gun from his coat, put a handkerchief over his mouth, then walked inside and shot the witness to death in front of several witnesses. Sims, no shrinking violet himself, was shocked by his partner's brazen act, and vowed never to work with McDonald again. McDonald was added to the Most Wanted list on April 1, 1976.

McDonald fled to Florida and went to work with another of his old partners, Johnny Martorano, on hits in Florida and Oklahoma. After receiving a tip, most likely from Whitey Bulger, McDonald was arrested in New York in 1982 while returning to Boston on a train. He had three Uzi submachines in his possession.

McDonald died a free man in 1997 at the age of 80.

WANTED BY THE FBI

INTERSTATE STOLEN PROPERTY; CONSPIRACY

JOSEPH MAURICE MC DONALD

DESCRIPTION

Born July 14, 1917, Boston, Massachusetts; Height, 5'9"; Weight, 165 to 175 pounds; Build, medium; Hair, gray; Eyes, blue; Complexion, fair; Race, white; Nationality, American; Occupations, laborer, truck driver; Scars and Marks, pockmark on right cheek, scar on right leg below knee; Social Security Number used, 022-05-6671.

CRIMINAL RECORD

McDonald has been convicted of unlawful carrying of firearm and assault and battery with a deadly weapon.

CAUTION

MC DONALD REPORTEDLY IN THE PAST HAS EXCHANGED SHOTS WITH ARRESTING OFFICERS AFTER ESCAPE FROM A CORRECTIONAL INSTITUTION. CONSIDER ARMED AND EXTREMELY DANGEROUS.

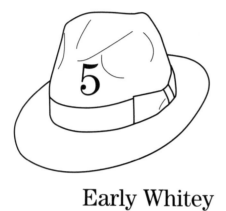

Early Whitey

From his tiny prison cell at the federal penitentiary in Tucson, Whitey Bulger continues to claim that he was not a "rat," not an informant for the FBI or other law-enforcement organizations.

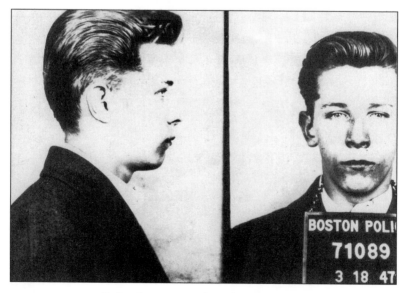

Earliest known mug shot of Whitey Bulger

At trial however, the FBI produced more than 700 pages of his informant file, all of which Whitey claimed were falsified after 1975, when he was added to the Bureau's roster of "Top-Echelon Informants."

But in reality, Whitey's career as a Mob canary went back much further, all the way to 1956. After Whitey's arrest, in return for fingering his partners in a multi-state bank-robbing gang, the feds agreed not to prosecute Whitey's moll.

She was Jacquie McAuliffe, a married woman separated from her steelworker husband. She was blonde, two years older than Whitey, and by all accounts a real knockout. And like most of the Bulger family's associates, she eventually got a state job, in the state Department of Revenue. McAuliffe died at Cape Cod Hospital in December 2010 at the age of 83.

WHITEY JOINED the Air Force in 1948 and was a discipline problem throughout his entire tour of duty. At one point, even before his arrest on statutory rape charges in Montana, his commanding officer was trying to separate him from the service on grounds of a fraudulent enlistment. But to the chagrin of the brass, Whitey had never been convicted of anything in Boston.

AlP 342.03
Subject: Fraudulent Enlistment   22 Jun 49

353BS   7th Ind   DCS/hgc

353d Bombardment Squadron, 301st Bombardment Group, Medium, Smoky Hill Air
    Force Base, Salina, Kansas, 11 August 1949

    TO: Commanding Officer, 301st Bombardment Group, Medium, Smoky Hill Air
         Force Base, Salina, Kansas

        1. Pfc James J Bulger, AF 11182966, hereinafter referred to as
subject, was arrested 18 March 1947 by Boston Mass. Police. He was not
convicted of the charge, i.e. Robbery, Unarmed.

        2. Subject was arrested on or about 6 Jan 1948. The charge, Assault
with intent to rape was officially changed to Assult and Battery. Subject
convicted of Simple Assault. His sentence was a fine only.

        3. Subject is not believed to have enlisted fraudulently, by
virtue of section 32, Enlistment Record, United States. i.e. Subject
was not convicted of the Felony, Robbery Unarmed.

        4. Section 35, Enlistment Record, United States, states truly the
information contained.

        5. Believe subject should not be discharged, per par B, AF Reg
39-21, insofar as it states it will be the general policy to retain
individuals in the service, who, upon enlistment, concealed a
conviction not punishable by death or imprisonment for more than
one year.

        FOR THE COMMANDING OFFICER:

                                        DALE C SMITH
                                        2nd Lt, USAF
1 Incl   Personnel Officer.
n/c

    CAUTION: SPECIAL HANDLING REQUIRED

    This material contained ...
    Records ...
    to be used ...
    or dissemination ...
    the Bureau.

Whitey had dodged another bullet.

When he returned to Boston, Whitey went back to the penny-ante rackets of his youth—tailgating, rolling drunks and turning tricks as a male prostitute. But he soon fell in with a more ambitious group—bank robbers. Two of Whitey's fellow bank robbers were Ron Dermody and Billy O'Brien. Dermody appears in the chapter "The Departed."

Here is the U.S. attorney's description of the gang's bank-robbing spree:

Form No. USA-792
(Rev. Oct. 1955)

77600-X.

CONTENTS NOTED
JUL 1 9 1956
WARDEN'S OFFICE

REPORT ON CONVICTED PRISONER BY UNITED STATES ATTORNEY

Name **James J. Bulger, Jr.**   Court Docket No. 56-89-S, 56-90-S, **56-113-S, 56-130-S**

Offense **Armed bank robbery**   Viol: Title **18**   Sec. **2113,2113 a & d, 371**

Date sentenced **June 21, 1956**   Term imposed **20 years**

Fine: (Committed - Not Committed) **Not committed**   Plea **Guilty**

Maximum term and fine possible **75 years, $35,000. total**

Trial Judge **George C. Sweeney**   Defense Attorney **Theodore A. Glynn, Jr.**

District **Massachusetts**   City **Boston**

1. Give date and full details of offense committed, including any aggravating or
   mitigating circumstances. (Continue on separate sheet if necessary.)

Bulger on May 17, 1955 together with Ronald Dermody and Carl G. Smith
participated in the armed robbery of the Industrial National Bank,
Darlington Branch, Pawtucket, R. I. In participating in this robbery,
Bulger carried a 22 revolver and forced two employees of the bank to
lie on the floor during the course of the robbery. The get-away from
the robbery was accomplished by the use of a car stolen by three
participants just prior to the robbery. Amount stolen was $42,112.

On November 18, 1955 William L. O'Brien participated in the holdup of
the Highlands Branch of the Melrose Trust Company, Melrose, Mass.
Prior to the robbery O'Brien and Bulger had carefully looked over the
bank. On the day of the robbery they stole the car to be used in the
get-away from an MTA parking lot in East Boston. They then placed
their switch cars in the parking lot of the Roosevelt School in Melrose
and proceeded from there in the stolen car to the bank. Both O'Brien
and Bulger were armed and took part in forcing the employees and cus-
tomers of the bank to lie on the floor during the robbery. They then
left the bank in the stolen car and switched to their own cars at the
Roosevelt School in Melrose. Total amount stolen was $5,035.

On November 23, 1955 Bulger, together with Richard R. Barchard, participated in the armed holdup of the Woodmar Branch of the Hoosier
State Bank, Hammond, Indiana. He and Barchard had set up the robbery
of this bank earlier in the Fall of 1955 and made the trip from Boston
to Indiana on or about November 23rd for the express purpose of accomplishing this robbery. Both Bulger and O'Brien entered the bank.
Bulger held two pistols on the person in the bank while Barchard,
unarmed, scooped the cash out of the drawers.

Judge George Sweeney, who sentenced Whitey, was a close ally of Joseph P. Kennedy, the father of JFK. According to Seymour Hersh in *The Dark Side of Camelot*, in 1946 Sweeney tried to stop a Jewish buyer from acquiring Suffolk Downs over the much lower bid of Joe Kennedy, who wanted to pay 10 cents on the dollar. In chambers, when the Jewish businessman offered to write a brief outlining why he would be a better buyer, Sweeney told him not to bother.

"I may be wrong," the judge said, "but I am never in doubt."

Whitey was captured in early 1956 at the Reef Café in Revere while planning another bank robbery in Cam-

Teddy Glynn: Whitey's 1956 lawyer and future judge

bridge with an ex-con named John DeFeo. As noted above, Whitey quickly cut a deal with the prosecutors, ratting out his accomplices. That saved his bombshell girlfriend Jacquie McAuliffe, whose name is redacted below, from having to stand trail on charges of harboring a fugitive.

The most significant sentence is the last—Bulger "orally admitted" the names of his fellow robbers. But he would not have to testify against them, and could thus preserve the fiction that he was a "stand-up guy."

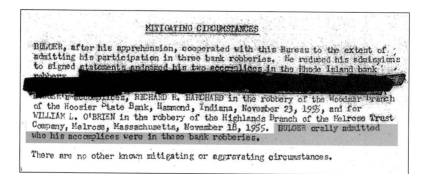

MITIGATING CIRCUMSTANCES

BULGER, after his apprehension, cooperated with this Bureau to the extent of admitting his participation in three bank robberies. He reduced his admissions to signed statements and named his two accomplices in the Rhode Island bank robbery.

▮▮▮▮▮ accomplices, RICHARD R. BARCHARD in the robbery of the Woodmar Branch of the Hoosier State Bank, Hammond, Indiana, November 23, 1955, and for WILLIAM L. O'BRIEN in the robbery of the Highlands Branch of the Melrose Trust Company, Melrose, Massachusetts, November 18, 1955. BULGER orally admitted who his accomplices were in these bank robberies.

There are no other known mitigating or aggravating circumstances.

THE FIRST OF THE bank robbers to be released from prison was Ron Dermody, who got out in early 1964.

During his eight years in prison, his girlfriend had taken up with another gangster, who was serving a state bit when Dermody was released.

At the time the gang war between the McLaughlins of Charlestown and the McLean gang of Winter Hill was raging out of control. One of the McLaughlins sought out Dermody, knowing that, as a long-absent Cambridge native, Dermody would not be recognized if he walked into one of the Winter Hill hangouts.

So Dermody was told that if he killed Buddy McLean, the McLaughlins, who were a power in Massachusetts prisons, would dispose of his romantic rival.

Ron Dermody

Dermody was convinced, and soon was driving up and down Broadway, looking for McLean, who bore a strong resemblance to Whitey's younger brother, Billy.

Billy Bulger

Buddy McLean

Of course, just as the Hill didn't recognize him, Dermody likewise didn't know Buddy McLean by sight. So he just opened fired on the first blond-haired man he saw. He wounded an innocent bystander.

Terrified, knowing he was now a marked man, Dermody reached out to the one man he thought he could trust—the FBI agent who had arrested him in 1956, H. Paul Rico. Rico, who lived in Belmont, told Dermody to drive to his hometown and he would meet him on the Belmont-Watertown line. A couple of hours later, as Dermody sat in a borrowed car, smoking a cigarette, a gunman approached him.

It was Buddy McLean.

After murdering Dermody, McLean was picked up by Rico, who had been using him as an informant for years. In-deed, there has been speculation that it was McLean who gave up Whitey in 1956, when the fugitive bank robber was arrested by Rico, despite having dyed his hair black as a disguise and chomping on a cigar whenever he was out in public in order to distort his facial features.

William O'Brien

After gunning down Dermody, McLean holed up in Rico's basement until the heat died down.

AS FOR O'BRIEN, he was no relation to the other William O'Brien, machine-gunned by the Winter Hill Gang in 1973.

O'Brien was also released from prison around 1965, and like Whitey and Dermody, quickly fell back into his old life of crime. In late 1966, he and several confederates were arrested for an armored-car robbery.

O'Brien, who at age 44 had taken up with a twentysomething girl, borrowed her car in early 1967 and drove to a secluded area in Dedham. His body was found the next day.

Whitey has never been publicly linked to O'Brien's murder. Indeed, his story seems much like the final days of novelist George V. Higgins' protagonist in *The Friends of Eddie Coyle*. But shortly before his death, Higgins said Coyle was a completely fictional character.

Dottie Barchard: gangster moll, had two children by O'Toole.

Before O'Toole, Dottie had been married to one of Whitey Bulger's bank-robbing gang, and later she took up with a lawyer whose car was blown up by the Mafia.

The Bulger Brothers circa 1965—Billy, Whitey and Jackie

A third member of the gang was Richard Barchard. His wife, Dottie, went on to become one of Boston's best-known molls of the 1950's and 1960s, hooking up with an string of plug uglies. She had two children by Spike O'Toole, who would later be murdered in Dorchester in 1973 by a Winter Hill hit crew, with Whitey Bulger at the wheel of the "boiler."

Whitey was released from Leavenworth in 1965. He soon obtained a no-show job as a janitor at the Suffolk County courthouse. (The late *Globe* sportswriter Will McDonough, Billy Bulger's first campaign manager in 1960, later claimed that he, and not Billy, had obtained that initial job for Whitey.)

By 1971, Whitey had thrown in with the Killeens, a gang of brothers who ran many of Southie's rackets out of a ginmill in the Lower End called the Transit Café. (It would soon be known as Triple O's.) Among other chores, Whitey handled the afternoon bets on dog races at Wonderland Track in East Boston. He was basically going nowhere in the underworld.

During his years in prison, Whitey had been watched over by the powerful House majority leader John McCormack of South Boston, who became Speaker in 1961. One of McCormack's closet allies in D.C. was FBI director J. Edgar Hoover.

George Killeen: murdered 1950

Donald Killeen: murdered 1972

John McCormack: House speaker

FBI director J. Edgar Hoover

After 42 years in Congress, McCormack finally retired in 1970. A few months after the Speaker's retirement, J. Edgar Hoover directly intervened with the Boston FBI office to bring Whitey into the fold as an informant, making him more or less immune from arrest, which was indeed what later happened.

Below, see Hoover's brief order to the Boston office on the "captioned source."

This was the description of Whitey that the Boston office quickly sent back to Hoover.

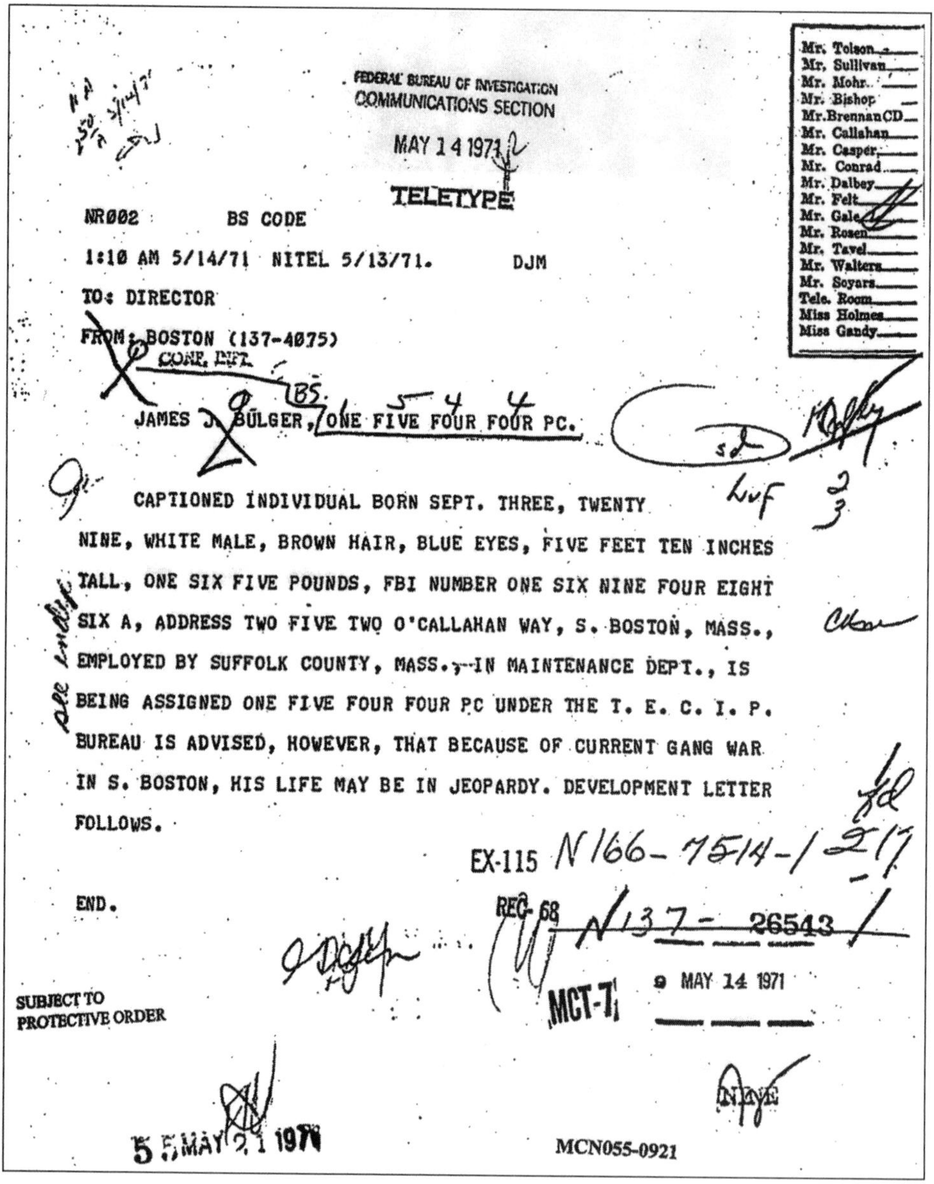

FEDERAL BUREAU OF INVESTIGATION
COMMUNICATIONS SECTION
MAY 14 1971
TELETYPE

Mr. Tolson
Mr. Sullivan
Mr. Mohr
Mr. Bishop
Mr. Brennan CD
Mr. Callahan
Mr. Casper
Mr. Conrad
Mr. Dalbey
Mr. Felt
Mr. Gale
Mr. Rosen
Mr. Tavel
Mr. Walters
Mr. Soyars
Tele. Room
Miss Holmes
Miss Gandy

NR002 BS CODE

1:10 AM 5/14/71 NITEL 5/13/71. DJM

TO: DIRECTOR

FROM: BOSTON (137-4075)

JAMES J. BULGER, ONE FIVE FOUR FOUR PC.

CAPTIONED INDIVIDUAL BORN SEPT. THREE, TWENTY NINE, WHITE MALE, BROWN HAIR, BLUE EYES, FIVE FEET TEN INCHES TALL, ONE SIX FIVE POUNDS, FBI NUMBER ONE SIX NINE FOUR EIGHT SIX A, ADDRESS TWO FIVE TWO O'CALLAHAN WAY, S. BOSTON, MASS., EMPLOYED BY SUFFOLK COUNTY, MASS., IN MAINTENANCE DEPT., IS BEING ASSIGNED ONE FIVE FOUR FOUR PC UNDER THE T. E. C. I. P. BUREAU IS ADVISED, HOWEVER, THAT BECAUSE OF CURRENT GANG WAR IN S. BOSTON, HIS LIFE MAY BE IN JEOPARDY. DEVELOPMENT LETTER FOLLOWS.

END.

EX-115 N166-7514-1-2
REC-68 N137-26543
MAY 14 1971
MCT-7

SUBJECT TO PROTECTIVE ORDER

5 MAY 21 1971

MCN055-0921

With H. Paul Rico retired, the task of reeling Whitey in fell to Rico's former partner Dennis Condon of Charlestown.

What follows is a summation of Condon's two interviews with Whitey, including Whitey's self-serving accounts of the gang war in Southie, neglecting, for instance, to mention that he was the actual killer of Donald McGonagle, and his misidentification of the hoodlum who had his nose bitten off. (It was Mickey Dwyer, not Mickey Maguire.)

DIRECTOR, FBI 6/14/71

SAC, BOSTON (P)

ReBulet, 5/25/71 and Bulet to Boston, 6/3/71.

Informant has been contacted on 5/13/71 and 6/7/71. He has furnished the following information:

WILLIAM O'SULLIVAN, who was recently killed in a gang war on Savin Hill Avenue, Dorchester, Mass., had been closely associated with JAMES "WHITEY" BULGER. O'SULLIVAN had had a reputation as a "tough guy" because he had been closely associating with FRANK SALEMME and STEVE FLEMMI, both UFAP Fugitives. He said that about the time that FLEMMI and SALEMME fled the Boston area after having been indicted for a gangland murder, DONALD KILEEN, a South Boston bookmaker, felt that it would be good protection for him to get O'SULLIVAN with him. He felt that O'SULLIVAN might help influence SALEMME and FLEMMI into not moving in to the South Boston bookmaker situation which they and LARRY BAIONE, LCN "lieutenant," were planning on doing. BULGER, with whom O'SULLIVAN became closely associated, was at about that same time working for KILEEN and helping him in his bookmaking operations. With SALEMME and FLEMMI removed from the Boston scene, "the organization's" thoughts about moving in to the South Boston bookmaking picture were shunted into the background.

KILEEN, however, was beginning to have problems with a young group of hold-up and B&E men led by one PAUL MC GONAGLE of South Boston, Mass. McGONAGLE's brother had been killed in gangland fashion about two years ago, and

2-Bureau
2-Boston

DMC
(4)

#4

A

he believed that DONALD KILEEN had contracted someone to kill him, PAUL MC GONAGLE, and, through a case of mistaken identity, MC GONAGLE's brother was killed. Additionally, KILEEN had had some trouble with MICKEY MAGUIRE, another associate of PAUL MC GONAGLE, and bit off his nose, necessitating plastic surgery.

During the Fall of 1970 and the Winter of 1970-1971, KILEEN, BULGER, and O'SULLIVAN began to get more pressure and trouble from PAUL MC GONAGLE and his associates, MICKEY MAGUIRE, PAUL MAHONEY, and PATRICK NEE.

In 2/71, one BUDDY ROACH, another close associate of PAUL MC GONAGLE, requested a meeting with WILLIAM O'SULLIVAN and JAMES "WHITEY" BULGER. At this meeting, ROACH told BULGER and O'SULLIVAN that he was going to "take out" DONALD KILEEN and that if O'SULLIVAN and BULGER stood in the way, they would also get killed. A violent argument ensued, ROACH threw a weapon and was thereafter shot by O'SULLIVAN. ROACH was seriously wounded and hospitalized. After this shooting, BULGER and O'SULLIVAN had expected retribution on the part of ROACH's associates. BULGER had been extremely cautious but O'SULLIVAN underestimated the group.

He said that in late 3/71, MC GONAGLE's group, but he could not say positively who was present with MC GONAGLE, waylaid O'SULLIVAN and killed him as he was entering his home on Savin Hill Avenue, Dorchester, Mass.

Informant advised that KILEEN, BULGER, and O'SULLIVAN did not wish to contact "the organization" to try to establish a peace in South Boston as they believe that once you let "the organization" feel you need their help, they thereafter take over the whole operation. He said that they also did not wish to contact the Somerville group under the leadership of "HOWIE" WINTERS because they felt that the young group from South Boston, with whom they were having trouble, was on good terms with WINTERS.

Informant advised that BULGER has been extremely careful since the murder of O'SULLIVAN and feels that he will be murdered if he lets his guard down. Informant

2

Finally, the FBI grew tired of Whitey's evasions and his obvious preoccupation with staying alive rather than reporting gangland gossip.

DIRECTOR, FBI   9/10/71

SAC, BOSTON   (C)

Re Boston letter to Bureau 6/14/71.

Contacts with captioned individual have been unproductive. Accordingly, this matter is being closed.

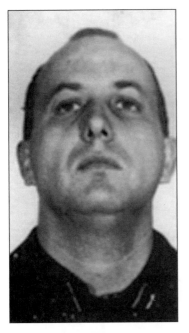

William O'Sullivan   Mickey McGuire

Paul Mahoney

Buddy Leonard

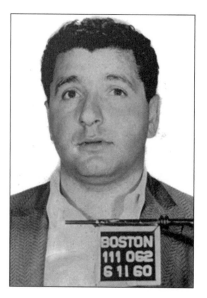

Louis Litif

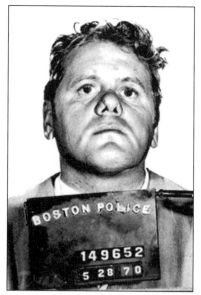

Mickey Dwyer

Even though he wasn't officially an FBI informant, Whitey still occasionally talked with the G-men. In 1973, after the murder of his old boss Donald Killeen, Whitey consolidated his hold on the South Boston rackets, and the FBI cautioned him that he was moving too fast, even shaking down one of his longtime gay lovers, Hank Geraghty, who owned the Pen Tavern. Geraghty had even visited Whitey in Leavenworth, and the two Southie hoodlums had both shared the sexual favors of gay Hollywood heartthrob Sal Mineo when Mineo was performing in a Boston nightclub shortly after Whitey's release from prison in 1965. After the warning from the FBI to slow down, Whitey spent less time on his Southie shakedowns and began spending more time with his new colleagues at their garage in Somerville.

By 1975, he was one of the leaders of the Winter Hill Gang, described by the soon-to-be-murdered Richie Castucci as an "animal." He had also "disappeared" two of his longtime foes in the rival Mullens gang, Paulie McGonagle and Tommy King. His brother was closing in on the presidency of the Massachusetts State Senate.

Whitey Bulger was about to officially partner up with fellow serial killer Stevie Flemmi to become a "Top Echelon" informant for the FBI.

In short, Whitey Bulger was about to become "Whitey Bulger."

Mugshots and More

Sam "Big Nose" Cufari: Springfield Mafioso

Gerry Ouimette: RI mobster, doing life, published
author, calls Howie Carr "The Trashman"

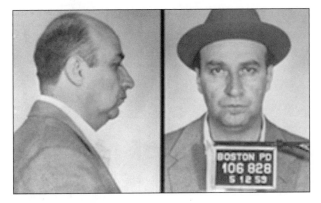

Sonny Boy Rizzo: longtime boss of Revere

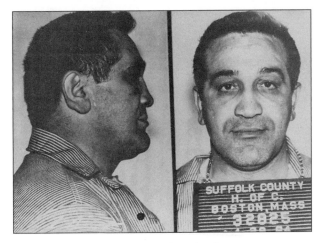

Sal Caeserio: North End enforcer

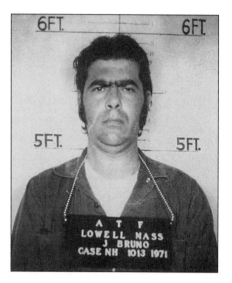

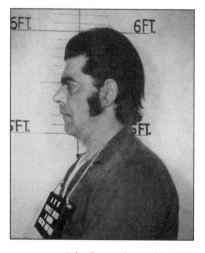

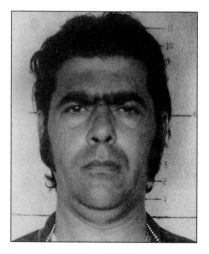

John Bruno: busted by ATF in $35,000 meat theft in Lowell 1971

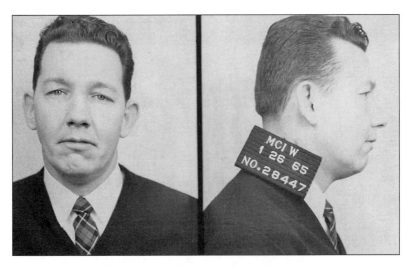

Jimmy Sims: future Winter Hill boss, now "missing"

Boston Mafia boss Joe Lombardo, before he retired in 1950

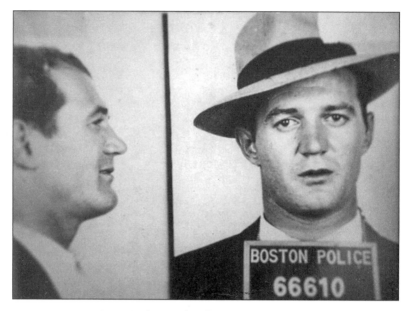

James Makris: Nashua bookie, arrested 1957

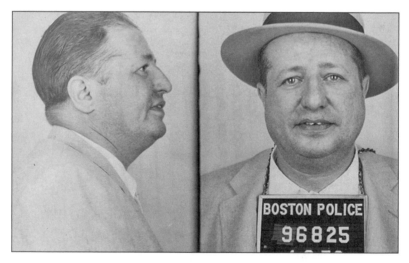

Harry Clayton: Brookline bookie

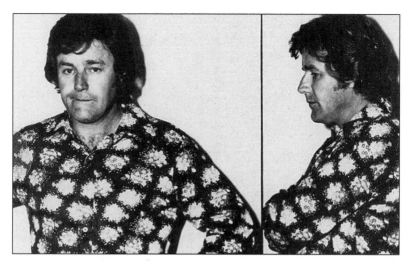

Frank McPartland: Nice shirt. Why the frown?

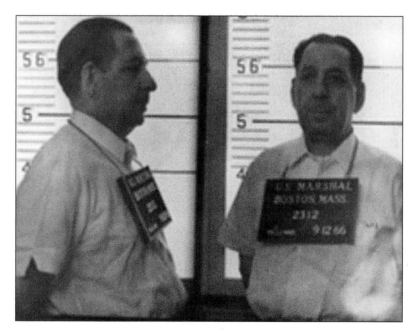

Eliott Price: made bets in Vegas for Winter Hill

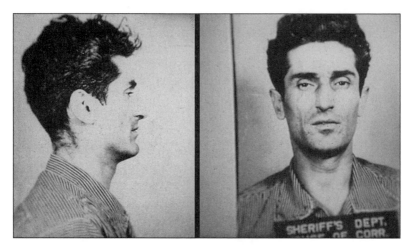

Bernard Zinna: slain 1969, robbed Mafia card games

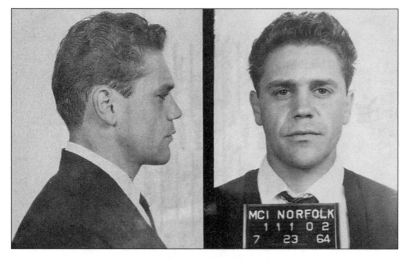

Angelo Mercurio. Famous quote: "I advocate the lam. Everybody run away."

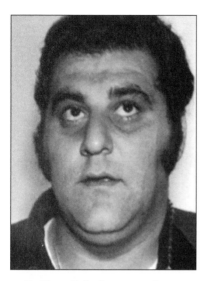

Fat Tony Ciulla: horse-race fixer

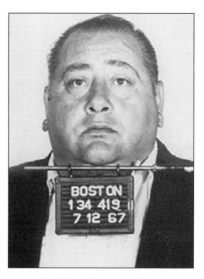

Fat Vinny Teresa: author
of *My Life in the Mafia*

Guido St. Laurent: founded
N.E.G.R.O.—New England Grass
Roots Organization. Blind ex-con,
murdered in Mattapan 1968

Ronald Hicks: witness to St. Laurent
slaying, murdered by Johnny Martorano

Abe Sarkis: Boston gambling czar   Anthony C. Ventura: Framingham, MA

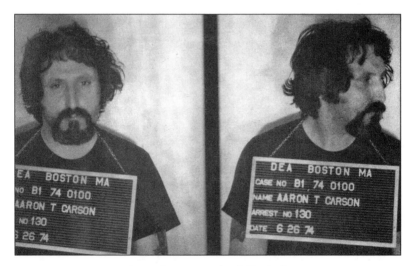

Aaron Carson: another DEA pinch

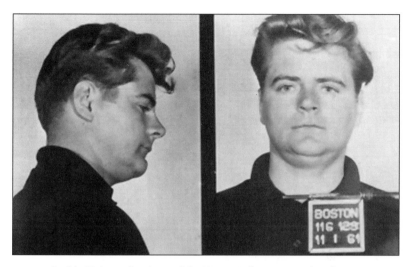

Buddy McLean: first boss of the Winter Hill gang, murdered 1965

Steve Flemmi: "the Rifleman"

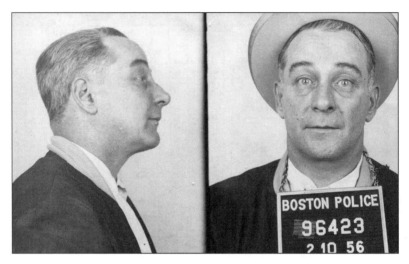

Harold Hannon: friend of the McLaughlins, murdered 1964

Richard Devlin: hitman, murdered 1994

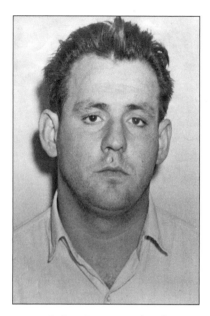

Carlton Eaton: murdered
by Joe Barboza 1964

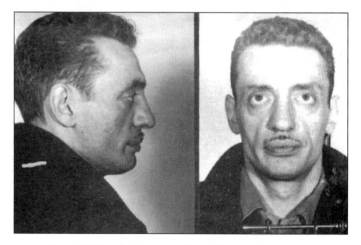

Frank Balliro: died in car accident, New Year's Eve 1968

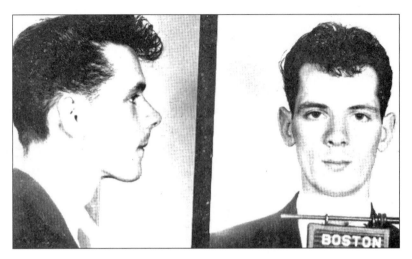

John Locke: McLaughlin gang member from Charlestown

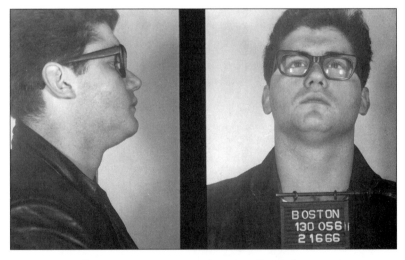

William Fopiano: another Mob author: *The Godson*. Dead.

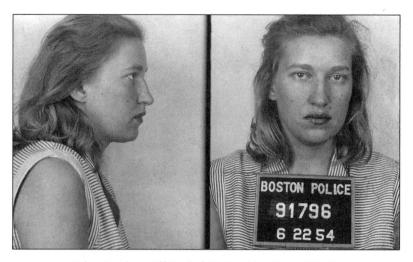

Helen Pouskas: girlfriend of Brinks robber Specs O'Keefe

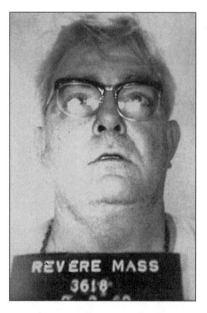

Arthur Ventola: owner of Arthur's
Farm, nationally known fencing
operation in Revere; once featured
in *Life* magazine as a hangout
for Boston pro athletes

Bernie McGarry: major Boston
layoff gambling czar

Deke Chandler: associate of
the Campbell Bros., murdered
in love triangle 1977

Frank Scibelli "Skyball:" boss of Mafia in Springfield,
where the cops took three mugshots

Anthony Scibelli, Jr.: another member of the family

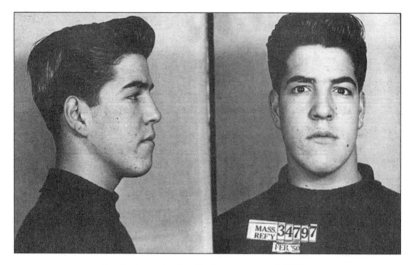

Joe Barboza: before he became a serial killer

Alvin Campbell, older of the Campbell
brothers, ran Roxbury, allied with
Johnny Martorano, now dead

Joseph Savitch, briefly New Bedford crime boss; remains
found in Aroostock County, Maine 1994

Lou Alexander: Joe Savitch's partner,
suffered same fate

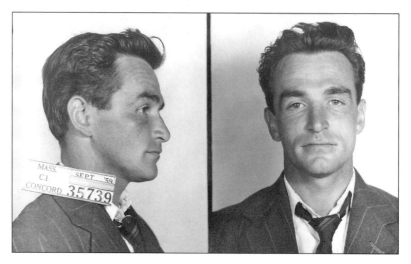

Joseph Brazil: Charlestown bank robber, murdered 1971

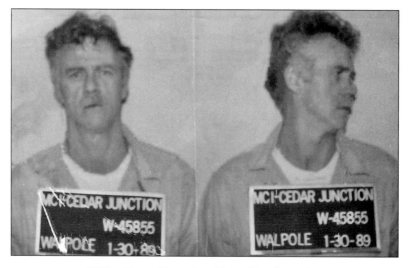

William Barnoski murdered Lowell bookie Jackie
McDermott 1988, died serving his sentence in 2013

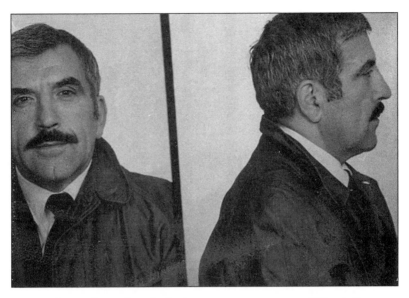

George Kattar: loanshark whose company was named "Piranha"

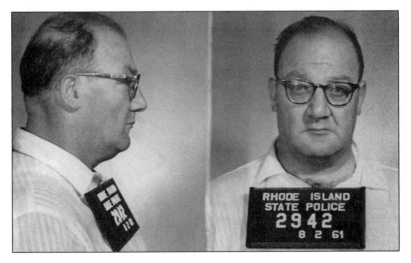

Alfred Rossi: Providence fence known as "The Blind Pig"

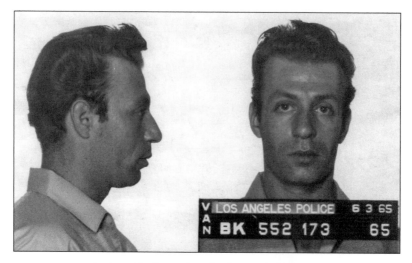

Anthony Stathopoulos after he wisely fled to LA

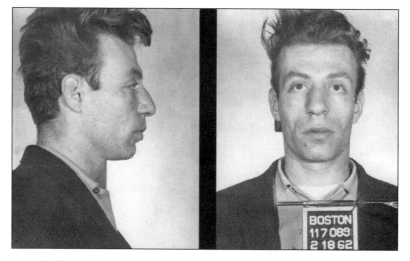

Stathopoulos was supposed to be killed with Teddy Deegan in 1965

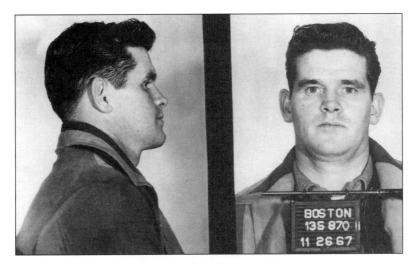

Arthur Doe, Sr.: father of Butchie Doe

Arthur "Butchie" Doe, Jr.: the infamous
Townie criminal of the 1980s

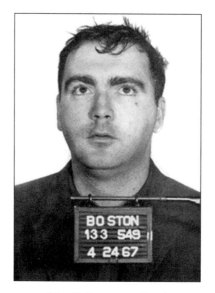

Brian Halloran: murdered
by Whitey 1982

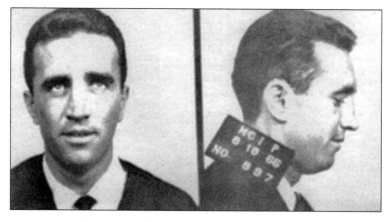

Daniel Moran: murdered Sal Sperlinga 1980, now serving life

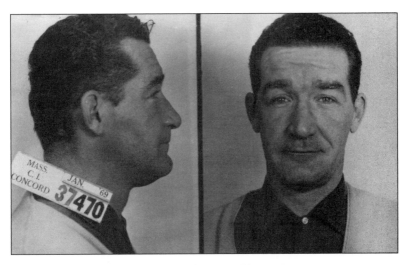

David Glennon: "missing from usual haunts" since 1971

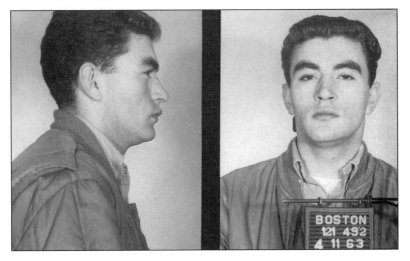

Dido Vaccari: one-time friend of Joe Barboza

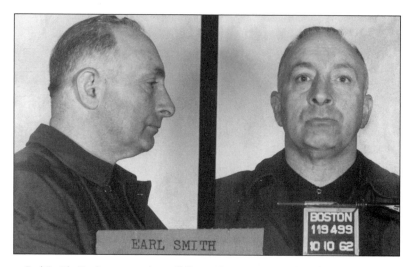

Earl Smith: Roxbury, associate of Wimpy Bennett, set up Punchy McLaughlin for unsuccessful hit in 1964, still active into the 1970s

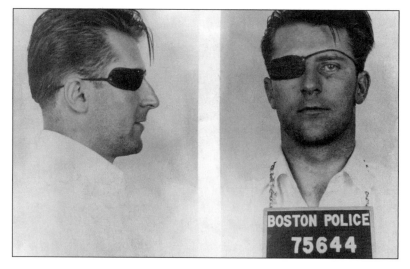

Francis Smith: versatile Boston gangster

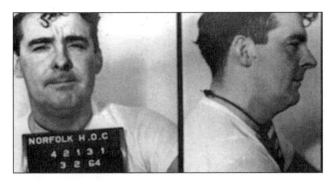

Francis X. Murray: nicknamed "Gaga"

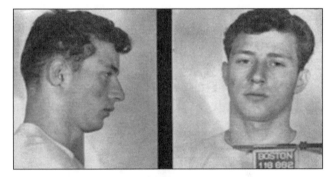

Frank A. Imbruglia: East Boston mobster,
"The Man with the Pretty Face"

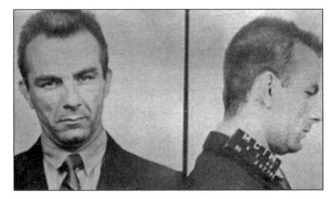

James N. Chalmas: Joe Barboza visited him
in San Francisco right before he was hit

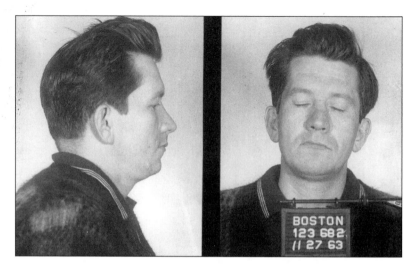

James "Spike" O'Toole: McLaughlin gang member, murdered
leaving Eddie Connors' bar in Dorchester 1973

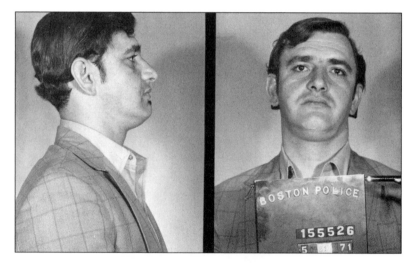

John Chodor: Mafia associate

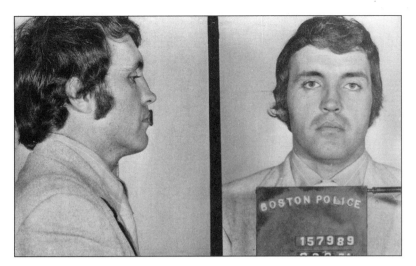

John Robichaud: murdered by Winter Hill 1973

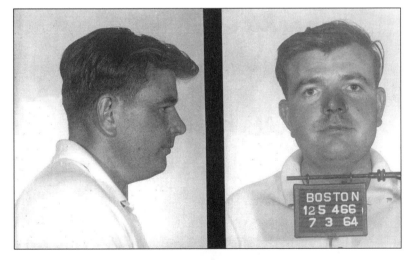

John Shackelford: Charlestown hood, nicknamed "Maxie,"
now reportedly living in Oklahoma

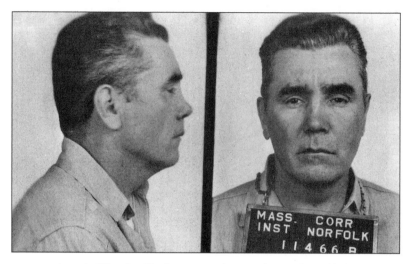

Joseph O'Rourke: Charlestown mobster nicknamed "Rockball"

Mike Caruana, reportedly buried in
Connecticut under tons of concrete

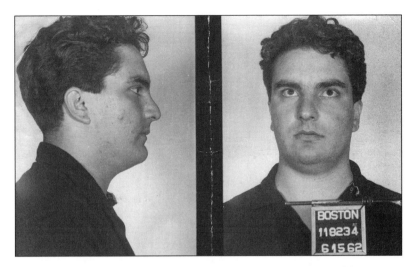

Nicholas Femia: Barboza hitman shot to death during East Boston robbery 1983; was a top suspect in 1978 Blackfriars slayings of five men

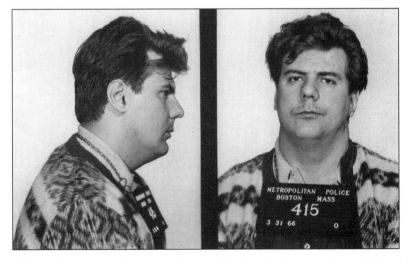

William Geraway: convicted murderer, author, *There's a $50,000 Price on My Head*

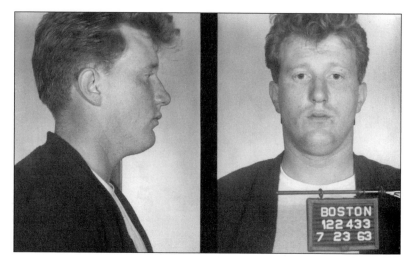

Red Clemens of Charlestown

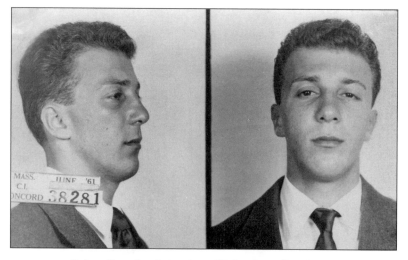

Robert Donati: twin brother of Richard, murdered 1990

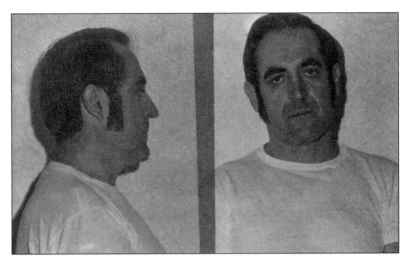

Robert Gallinaro: major Winter Hill bookie

Romeo Martin: murdered
by Joe Barboza 1965

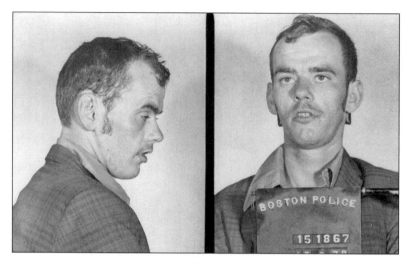

Ronald Hogan: one of five South Boston brothers

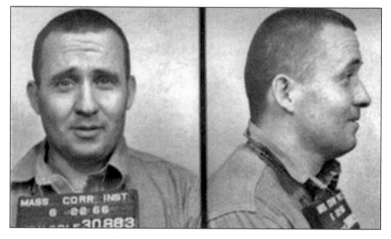

Tommy Ballou: Charlestown stevedore, murdered 1969

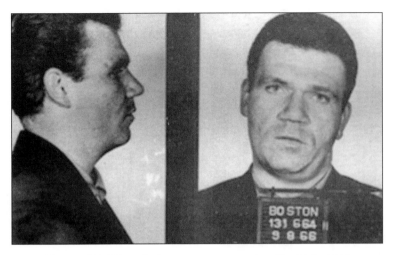

Thomas J. DePrisco: Barboza gangster, murdered by Mafia 1966

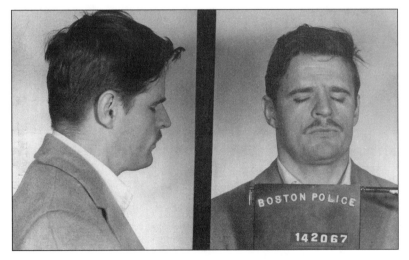

Walter Elliot: killed in escape attempt at MCI-Walpole, 1972

Joseph Russo: Mafia hitman,
murdered Joe Barboza 1976

Russo liked to design
his own clothes

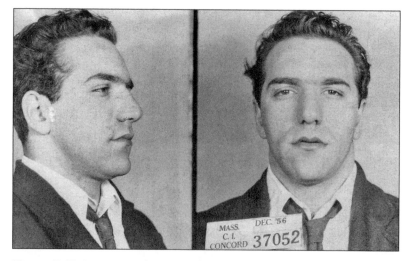

Vincent DeSiscio: partner of J.R. Russo, known together as "The Gold Dust Twins"

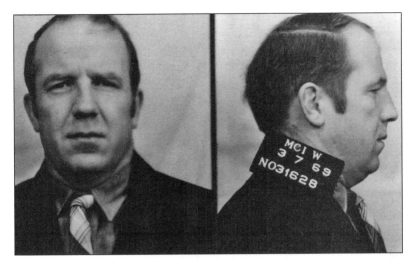

William Coyman: Winter Hill Gang

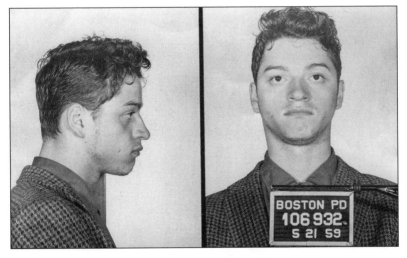

William Emma of Roxbury: Stevie Flemmi associate

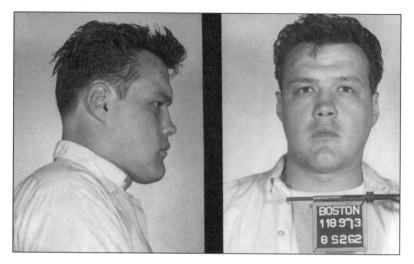

William Treannie: small-time South End hoodlum, murdered and dismembered 1964. Suitcases containing his body parts were left in the South End.

Wimpy Bennett: Roxbury hoodlum, murdered by Stevie Flemmi 1967

Wimpy after a court appearance in 1957

Early mugshot of Pat Linskey;
note the scar on his neck

Linskey, in his later role
as enforcer for Whitey

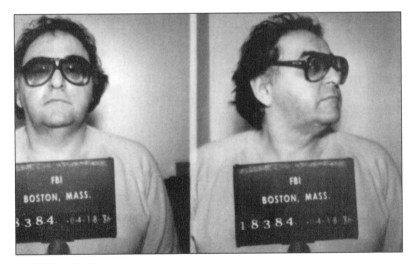

Anthony Nastasi, aka Nada: visitor to Doghouse

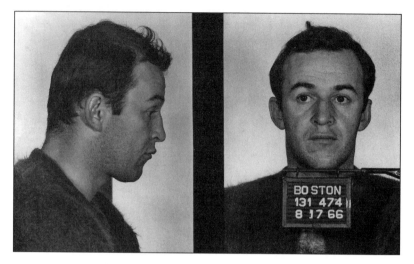

James Angiulo, aka Jimmy Jones: a nephew

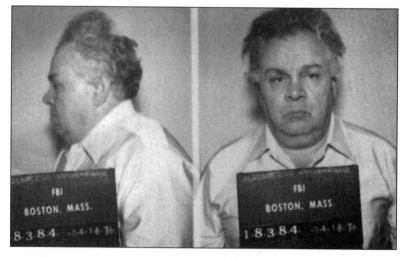

Joseph Candelino, aka Candy: visitor to Doghouse

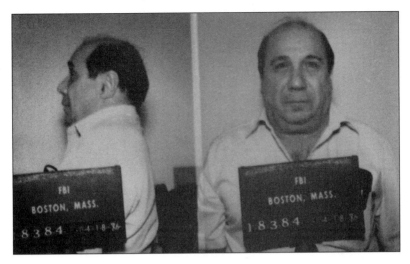

Mario Corrente: visitor to Doghouse

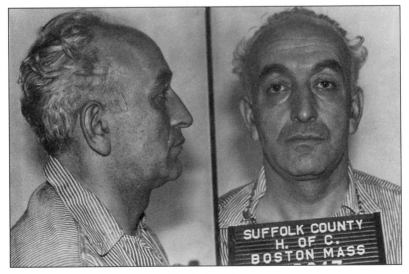

Nicolo Angiulo

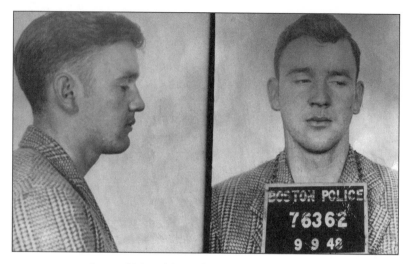

George McLaughlin: still in state prison at age 87

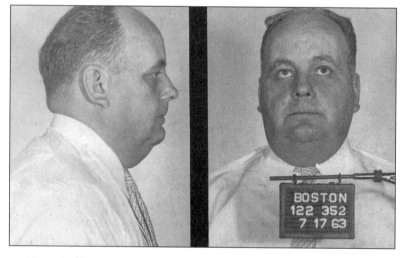

Henry Reddington: his fatal mistake was loaning Wimpy Bennett $25,000

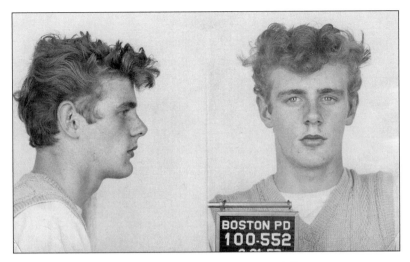

Peter Stenstrom: "Where's my comb?"

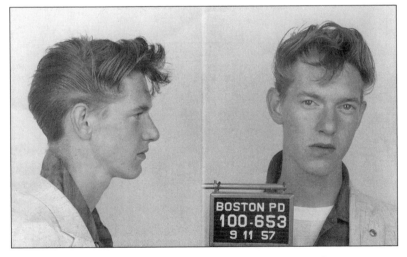

Wilfred Eden: charged with "being abroad in the night"

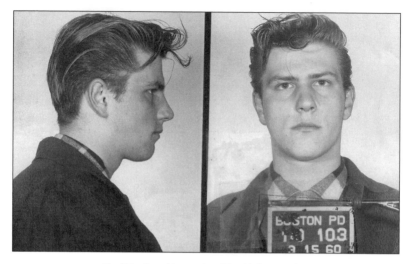

Paul Zanlewski: another "Kookie" wannabe

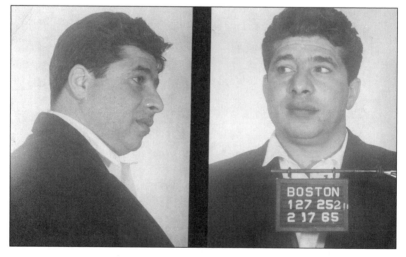

Paul James Bottari: "Look into the camera!"

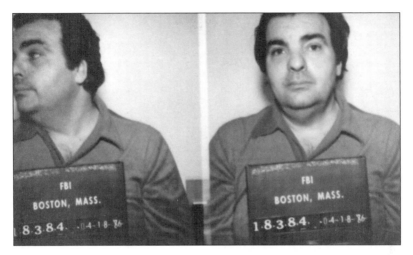

Anthony Firicano: aka "Gunga Din"

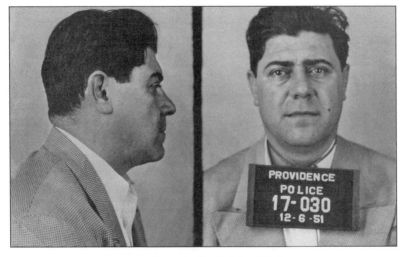

Henry Cipriano: Rhode Island Mafia

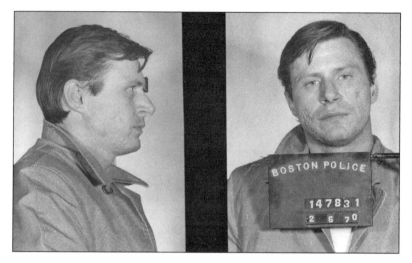

Robert Wilson: a true plug ugly from Southie

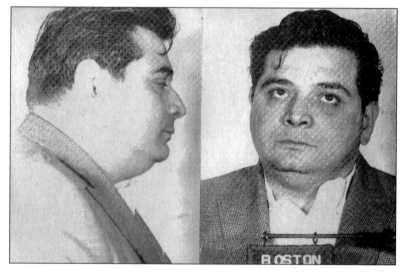

Benedicto Oddo took draft physical for look alike Johnny Martorano and failed

Jimmy Martorano
in the disco era

Jimmy Martorano:
Johnny's younger brother

Arrested Again

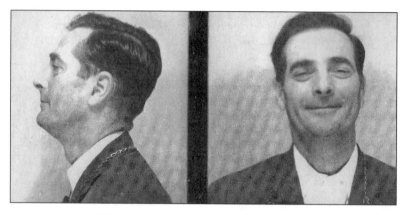

Milton Powers always smiled for his mug shot.

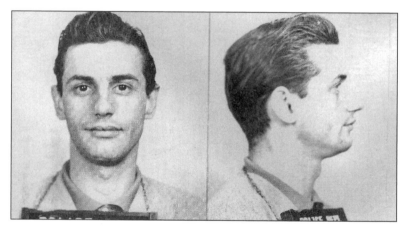

Bobby Carrozza: J. R. Russo's half-brother

William Kelley: still on death row in Florida

Teddy Green: bank robber

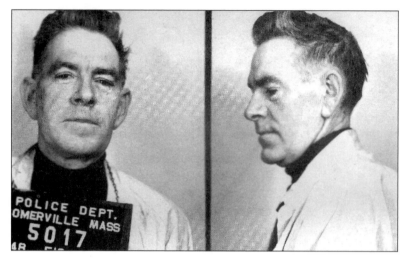

John Kearns, like father. . .

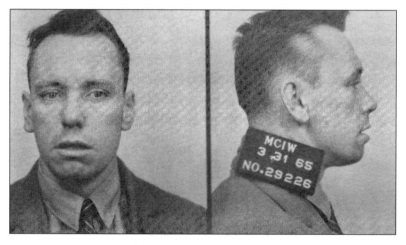

. . .like son, James Kearns

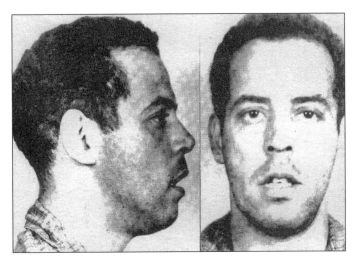

Donald Barboza: Joe's older brother

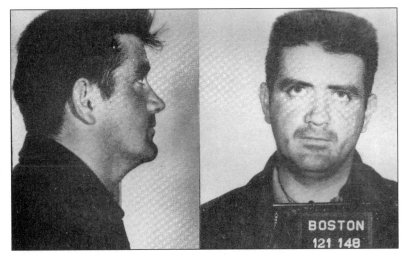

Leo Gillis

Roy Thomas: "In Town"

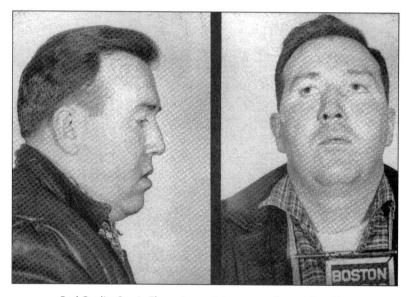

Red Conlin: Stevie Flemmi associate reportedly murdered by
his in-laws, 1971 (the in-laws were acquitted at trial)

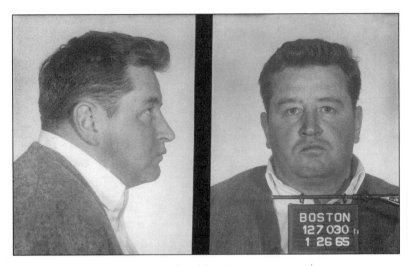

Dan Murphy

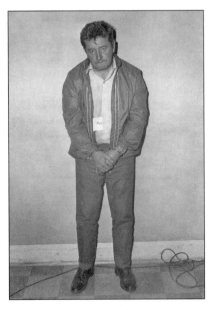

Dan Murphy

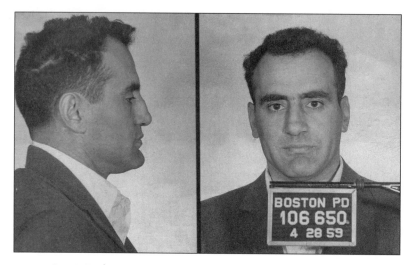

Connie Frizzi: quit Barboza's gang to join Mafia; good career move

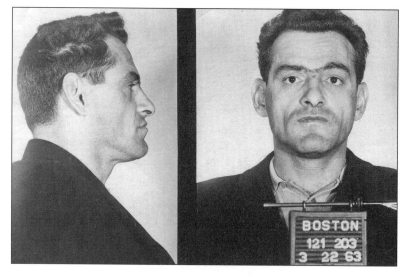

Guy Frizzi: Connie's kid brother

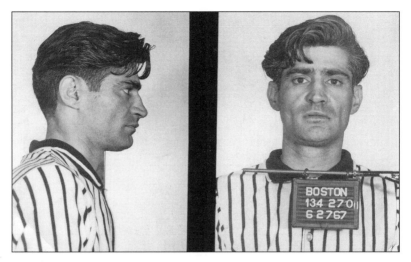

Edward Spagnuolo: this is not Spucky

James Murphy: by 1972, ducktails were out, sideburns were in

Joseph Franchi: Providence, RI

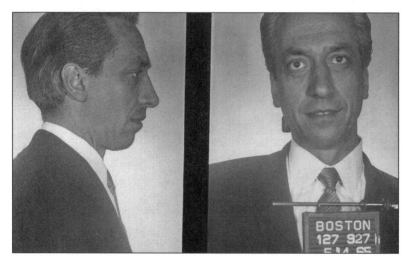

Russell Saia

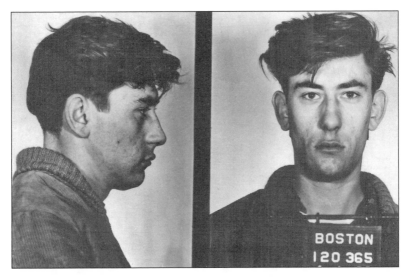

Tim McDougall

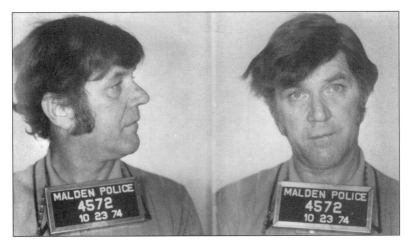

John Nickerson: "wears a wig"

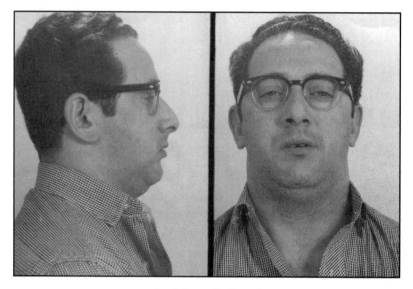

Frank Otero: "In Town"

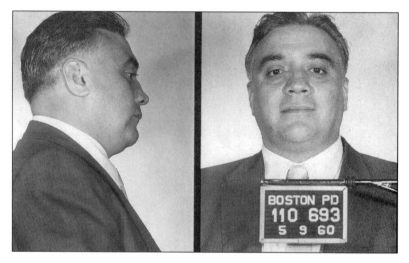

Jerry Iandoli: "In Town"

Scenes of the Crimes

Charlestown gunmen Stevie and Connie Hughes
are escorted into Boston police headquarters.
Soon after, in May 1966, Connie would be
wishing he had a police escort, as he was
hunted down by a Winter Hill hit squad.

Connie was ratted out by Brian Halloran, who
would later be murdered by Whitey.

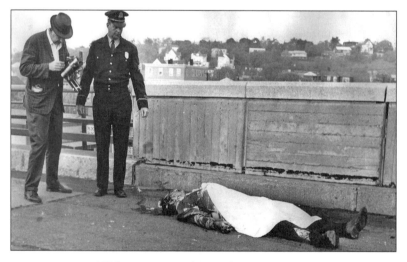

MDC cops getting photos of Connie's corpse

Nothing to see here folks, just another gangland hit…

A few days later, Stevie "Informant" Flemmi reported his take on the Hughes hit to corrupt FBI agent H. Paul Rico.

Informant advised that CORNELIUS HUGHES, who was murdered on 5/25/66 in Revere, Mass., had previously been around Dearborn Square, Roxbury, obviously in an effort to try to set him (informant) up for a "hit" and that the fact that CONNIE is now deceased is not displeasing to him.

Informant was asked if he had an idea who committed the murder and he advised that "he had an excellent idea who committed the murder" but it would be better if he did not say anything about the murder.

Informant did say, however, that LARRY BAIONE allegedly gave $5,000 to STEVIE HUGHES, CONNIE's brother, to be given to CONNIE's wife.

Informant advised that BAIONE definitely has "got to go." The only thing is that suspicion has to be thrown on to some other group. Informant advised that it is

Now Stevie Hughes was at the top of the Winter Hill Hit Parade. He got his as he was riding shotgun in a car driven by veteran Boston hoodlum Sammy Lindenbaum in October 1965.

Stevie and Sammy won't be down for breakfast.

Again, FBI agent Rico records the reaction of his ace informant Stevie Flemmi:

> Informant advised that since STEVIE HUGHES was murdered that the entire city is much more at ease. Informant made the comment that SAMMY LINDENBAUM, who was with STEVIE HUGHES at the time of the murder, should have known better than to be with STEVIE HUGHES, as it was obvious that STEVIE HUGHES eventually had to be "hit."
>
> (It should be noted that informant had previously advised that STEVIE HUGHES had been marked for a hit.)

Punchy McLaughlin's funeral in Canton 1965.

Police investigate car where George
Ashe was murdered in 1965.

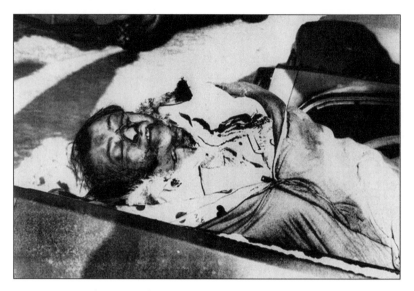

FBI informant Richie Castucci: murdered by FBI informants
Whitey Bulger and Stevie Flemmi

Richie Castucci: one of the owners
of the infamous Ebb Tide
on Revere Beach

Teddy Deegan: dead in a Chelsea alley, the screwdriver he was
planning to use to break into the bank lying beside him

Teddy Deegan: with
six weeks to live

Ronald Cassesso: one of Deegan's
killers, died in prison

Wilfred R. French: another of
Deegan's killers, paroled

Record reporter Jack Wharton checks out car in which
Rocco DiSeglio was slain (See "The Departed," page 46)

Sonny Shields was acquitted of
William Bennett's murder

Bill Stewart: Boston police detective
and hitman, also acquitted of
Billy Bennett murder

William Bennett: the last of the three
brothers murdered in 1967, lies
against Mattapan snow bank

Anthony D'Agostino: one of
Buddy's "bodyguards" that night

Rico Sacramone: the other
McLean "bodyguard," on his
way back to prison

The car Buddy McLean was sitting in when
he was murdered, October 1965

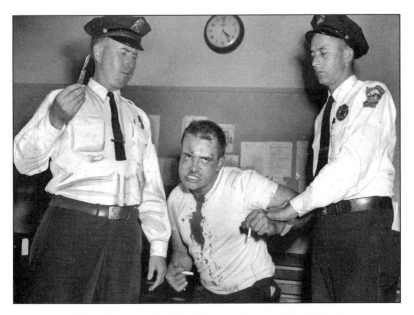

Walter Bannon, aka "Two Cigarette" Bannon. He stabbed
the cop on the left with his pocket knife.

If these two "Kookie" wannabes
had spent as much time planning
the crime as they did combing
their hair, we might not have
this photograph from 1958.

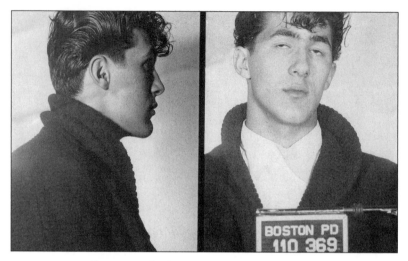

Chico Amico had a great ducktail haircut until…

…he ran into a Mafia hit crew as he was leaving a nightclub in Revere.

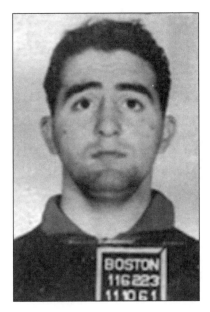

Patsy Fabiano: member of
Joe Barboza gang

Barboza pal found slain in gangland fashion

An underworld "songbird" who teamed with Joseph (Barboza) Baron nine years ago in testifying before a federal grand jury probing organized crime, was found shot to death yesterday in the North End.

The body of Patrick J. "Patsy" Fabiano, 32, of Puritan ln., Swampscott, was discovered slumped in the front seat of his car in a family-owned parking lot on North st.

He had been shot at least four times in the head at close range, police said.

Fabiano's death follows that of Barboza (Baron) who was gunned down in gangland fashion on Feb. 11, in San Francisco.

Law enforcement officials yesterday linked both killings to gangland vengeance for the role they played in providing federal authorities with their first solid information on the inner workings of the New England family of organized crime—the Cosa Nostra.

murder" charges involving the deaths of two Rhode Island brothers.

Fabiano, who had been a minor underworld figure and close friend of Barboza, agreed to become a government witness in 1967 after he learned from Suffolk County Dist. Atty. Garrett H. Byrne that he had been "marked for death" by his gangland associates.

He was convicted of a gun carrying charge in 1967 and sentenced to 3 to 5 years at Walpole State Prison. During his incarceration, he was moved from prison to prison and always kept under surveillance in protective custody.

Barboza's death was believed at first to be a "local hit"–and not related to his past criminal activities in the Boston area.

But yesterday, when word of Fabiano's murder surfaced, Inspector Stephen Mox of the San Francisco Police Dept. called Boston Police and informed them he had information which linked the two deaths to gangland vengeance.

BODY of Patrick J. "Patsy" Fabiano, discovered slumped in car in North End.
Staff Photo by Gene Dixon

Fabiano was slain a few weeks after his old boss in 1976

The bodies of Tash Bratsos and Tommy DePrisco were
left in the backseat of Tash's Cadillac in 1966.

The bodies are removed to the mortuary

Andrew Von Etter: another hood who
ended up in the trunk of his car...

...which had vanity license plates with his initials, AVE

"Phone call for Mr. Connors"

Messages from the Commissioner

Nobody writes memos like this anymore. If they did, they wouldn't have a job for long. The Commissioner was not politically correct, to say the least. Check out the message from Feb. 27, 1967, (page 183) in which, he castigates a decision of the U.S. Supreme Court.

That is not allowed in Massachusetts anymore, unless maybe it's *Citizens United.* And who are these "drug addicts" he's referring to? These are the people who patronize the "marijuana dispensaries" soon to be popping up all over the Commonwealth.

Let's hope Commissioners Richard R. Caples and L.L. Laughlin are no longer around to see what has become of their beloved state.

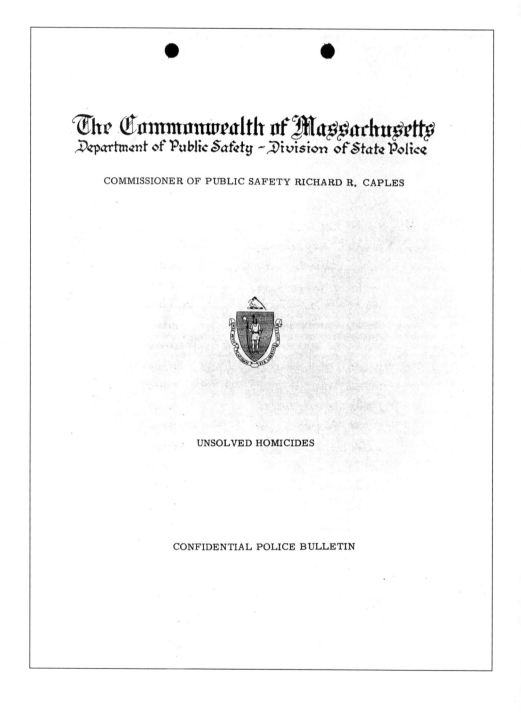

The Commonwealth of Massachusetts
Department of Public Safety – Division of State Police

COMMISSIONER OF PUBLIC SAFETY RICHARD R. CAPLES

UNSOLVED HOMICIDES

CONFIDENTIAL POLICE BULLETIN

UNSOLVED HOMICIDES - CONFIDENTIAL POLICE BULLETIN

5- 4-64	BENJAMIN, Francis R.	Boston
5-12-64	NICHOLSON, Russell C.	Wilmington
7-23-64	COLICCI, Paul J.	Quincy
7-23-64	BISESI, Vincent A.	Quincy
8-20-64	HANNON, Harold R.	(State) Boston
8-20-64	DELANEY, Wilfred T.	Boston
9- 3-64	LOWRY, Leo C.	Pembroke
9- 4-64	DERMADY, Ronald P.	Watertown
9-25-64	EATON, Carleton	Malden
10-17-64	SACRAMONE, Anthony D.	Everett
11-24-64	HUBER, Edward P.	Hingham
12-28-64	ASH, George E.	Boston
1-10-65	MURRAY, John F.	Boston
1-15-65	RASMUSSEN, Robert J.	Wilmington
1-23-65	REDDINGTON, Henry F.	Weymouth
1-26-65	FRANCIONE, Joseph R.	Revere
3- 2-65	BARBIERI, John Jr.	Rehoboth
3-12-65	DEEGAN, Edward T.	Chelsea
4-12-65	CASSETTA, Peter A.	Maynard
5-20-65	FERGNANI, William E.	Tyngsborough
7- 9-65	MARTIN, Joseph R.	Revere

Sales of Handguns to Massachusetts Residents by
    Out-of-state Dealers

Index of Names Mentioned

UNSOLVED HOMICIDES - CONFIDENTIAL POLICE BULLETIN

SECOND SUPPLEMENT - OCTOBER 18, 1966

8-22-65	DAVID, Edward	Boston
10-20-65	MC LAUGHLIN, Edward J.	Boston
10-30-65	MC LEAN, James	Somerville
11-15-65	PALLADINO, Robert T.	Boston
11-15-65	DI STASIO, Raymond	Revere
11-15-65	O'NEILL, John B.	Revere
4-24-66	SIDLAUSKAS, David M.	Quincy
4-26-66	VERANIS, Anthony	Quincy
5-25-66	HUGHES, Cornelius	Revere
6-16-66	DI SEGLIO, Rocco	Topsfield
9-23-66	HUGHES, Stephen	Middleton
9-23-66	LINDENBAUM, Samuel	Middleton
9-28-66	JACKSON, John W.	Boston

The Commonwealth of Massachusetts

Department of Public Safety
1010 Commonwealth Avenue, Boston, Mass. 02215
December 5, 1966

MASSACHUSETTS CRIMINAL INFORMATION BUREAU

Dear Chief:

Enclosed are some additional photographs and registration numbers that may be of interest to you and the members of your Department. Additional copies may be had upon request to the supervisor of the Massachusetts Bureau of Identification.

Your attention is invited to the statutes covering the furnishing of fingerprints and photographs to the M.B.I. of persons arrested upon process or for felonious offenses. (Please see Chapters 263, S la; 147, S 4a, 4b, 4c and 127, S. 23, 25 and 29). It is suggested you may wish to discuss this with the members of your Department to insure that these statutes are being complied with. The M.B.I. is a depository of fingerprints, photographs and information concerning criminals, parolees, etc., exclusively for the use of law enforcement officers. It is only as good and helpful as all police make it by submitting their contributions.

Indications are that there is an increase in the number of safe jobs and many breaks in business establishments and private dwellings. In the latter, personal firearms have been stolen and it can be expected that these will turn up in criminal activities at a later date. We have also noted an increase in the amount of tailgating of trucks. This is particularly true of those hauling meat.

The following Chapter 140, S. 96, covering small loans, is set forth for your full information:

> "No person shall directly or indirectly engage in the business of making loans of three thousand dollars or less, if the amount to be paid on any such loan for interest and expenses exceeds in the aggregate an amount equivalent to twelve per cent per annum upon the sum loaned, without first obtaining from the Commissioner of Banks a license to carry on said business in the town where the business is to be transacted."

It would be appreciated if you would be alert and report any information of drug addicts, particularly when observed in the vicinity of establishments that dispense drugs, doctors' offices and doctors' automobiles.

Once again we solicit your cooperation in submitting information to the Criminal Information Bureau. As we have pointed out in previous communications, this is established for the benefit of all law enforcement in order that we may be helpful to police departments by exchanging information contained in our files.

Sincerely yours,

L. L. Laughlin
Commissioner

LLL:ybs

Enclosure

The Commonwealth of Massachusetts
Department of Public Safety

1010 Commonwealth Avenue
Boston, Massachusetts 02215
August 27, 1965.

Dear Chief and Other Law Enforcement Officials:

A meeting was held on July 20, 1965, at my office with a committee of the Massachusetts Chiefs of Police Association and members of the Massachusetts State Police, at which time plans were formulated for disseminating to all police agencies, information concerning the recent so-called "gangland-type" murders in order to encourage the submission of all leads which, when gathered, could assist the investigations.

As a result of sending to each chief a preliminary outline of the offenses and victims involved, we have been able to add other associates and information to compile this "Blue Bulletin" as an insert to the regular Identification Bulletin of this Department.

This publication is intended to acquaint all law enforcement officers with basic information in an endeavor to identify and apprehend the persons responsible and to prevent further defiance of this type. As a reference pamphlet, the bulletin is certainly not all-inclusive. For more detailed information on the associates listed, or to learn where additional leads may fit in, you are encouraged to contact the investigating department or this office. It should be noted that in some cases those listed as associates could be deemed suspects, and no assumption should be made as to "friendly" associations.

Some of the murders which are often grouped as "gangland" have been omitted because of apprehensions or other reasons. As additional information is submitted by officers throughout the Commonwealth, it will not only be passed on to investigators, but is expected to be published as supplementary "Blue Bulletins", as necessary, through the same mailing list.

I am grateful for the assistance which has been given by all concerned in this pilot effort at concentrated cooperation in these crimes, and will welcome any suggestions which can aid in the extension of this program.

Very truly yours,

Richard R. Caples,
Commissioner of Public Safety

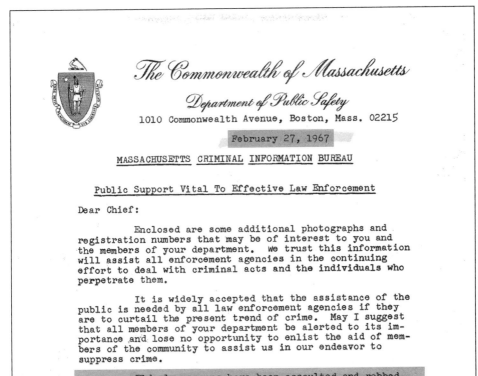

The Commonwealth of Massachusetts

Department of Public Safety

1010 Commonwealth Avenue, Boston, Mass. 02215

February 27, 1967

MASSACHUSETTS CRIMINAL INFORMATION BUREAU

Public Support Vital To Effective Law Enforcement

Dear Chief:

Enclosed are some additional photographs and registration numbers that may be of interest to you and the members of your department. We trust this information will assist all enforcement agencies in the continuing effort to deal with criminal acts and the individuals who perpetrate them.

It is widely accepted that the assistance of the public is needed by all law enforcement agencies if they are to curtail the present trend of crime. May I suggest that all members of your department be alerted to its importance and lose no opportunity to enlist the aid of members of the community to assist us in our endeavor to suppress crime.

Elderly persons have been assaulted and robbed on the public streets. Housebreaking and burglary are overtaxing enforcement capabilities. Holdups and robberies show no sign of decline. Unlawful possession of firearms is general in these holdups and robberies. Recently, a case involving the use of tear gas was reported. The distribution of counterfeit bills has been detected. Reports of safes being removed from the premises and found dismantled in rural areas have been increasing, together with reports of safes being cracked open on the premises.

Special attention should be directed towards violators of the drug and narcotic laws and most especially where they involve sale to school children.

A new type of hit and run crime has become evident. It is the situation where an individual is "hit" and his killers flee the scene. Victims have been found in all types of locations. The homicides have occurred as the result of shooting, strangling, drowning, decapitation,

- 2 -

stabbing and severe beatings. In most of these cases law enforcement officers have been severely handicapped by the lack of witnesses or other tangible evidence. This, coupled with recent decisions of the U. S. Supreme Court, have made convictions difficult to obtain.

There is every indication that until the public actively lends its efforts to the cause of effective law enforcement, we shall remain handicapped. Every effort should be exerted to develop public awareness of the threat presented to society by the malignant nature of criminal activities.

The Criminal Information Bureau was established for the use of all police departments of the Commonwealth. Information coming to your attention that would be valuable to other departments should be sent to the Bureau without delay.

Good information, with substantiative witnesses, is needed to bring about successful prosecutions. The police have many opportunities to bring this message to the community via local newspapers, various meetings, their everyday contact with citizens, local radio station broadcasts and television.

Every police officer should be instructed to solicit the full cooperation of all citizens in the community. Crime is of concern to us, to them, and to everyone in the entire country.

Sincerely,

L. L. Laughlin
Commissioner

LLL:amm

Enclosure

MASSACHUSETTS DEPARTMENT OF PUBLIC SAFETY   CONFIDENTIAL POLICE BULLETIN

INFORMATION IS SOUGHT ON THE FOLLOWING CRIMES:

U.S. Mail Truck Robbery, August 14, 1962

On the night of Tuesday, August 14, 1962 at about 8 PM, a U.S. Mail Truck was hi-jacked in the northbound lanes of State Route 3, near Plymouth, Mass., approximately 3 miles south of the intersection with U.S. Highway 44. The postal driver and guard were held captive until the truck was abandoned in the Randolph area, at the intersection of State Routes 128 and 28.

During the ride between the holdup and abandonment points, a distance of about 50 miles, the 16 pouches in the truck containing a total of $1,551,277. in currency were removed from the mail truck.

Skelly's Armored Station Wagon, Quincy, January 16, 1965

On Saturday, January 16, 1965, $31,000. in cash was taken from an armored station wagon in the parking lot of the Wheel House Diner on Hancock Street in Quincy. The driver and guards were having lunch in the diner and the vehicle was locked. One man seen leaving the diner shortly before the guards entered, and two men observed laboring under the hood of a parked car as the guards drove into the parking lot, may be involved.

Jewel Burglary, Worcester, April 14, 1965

On Wednesday, April 14, 1965, burglars entered the Diamond Jewelers, Inc., 421 Main Street, Worcester, by climbing a fire escape, entering a window, cutting through a door covered with chicken wire, and then lowering themselves by means of a rope into the jewelers premises. They took over $40,000. in diamonds and other jewelry, and $3,600. in cash.

Skelly's Armored Truck, Brookline, March 3, 1966

About 9 AM on March 3, 1966 while Skelly's Armored Truck was parked in front of the New England Food Fair on Harvard Street, Brookline making a delivery, a man with a guard's hat jumped into the truck and drove it away with $65,000.

Jewel Robbery, Boston, March 24, 1966

Shortly after 9 AM on March 24, 1966, two masked men carrying revolvers held up Cortell's Jewelry Store, Washington Street, Boston, and took $300,000. in uncut diamonds and other jewelry.

Armored Car Robbery, Concord, May 26, 1966

About 8:45 AM on May 26, 1966, three masked men carrying revolvers and one sawed-off shotgun held up an armored truck of the Armored Banking Service of Lynn at the General Radio Corporation in Concord, and took approximately $70,000.

Clothes Hi-Jack, Lawrence, June 6, 1966

At about 4 PM on June 6, 1966, a GMC Van Truck was hi-jacked in Lawrence and later recovered about 10 PM, same date, in Dracut with $50,000. worth of winter coats missing. The merchandise was owned by the Cape Ann Manufacturing Co. of Gloucester.

MASSACHUSETTS DEPARTMENT OF PUBLIC SAFETY   CONFIDENTIAL POLICE BULLETIN

Rehtstein Flour Co. Robbery, Charlestown, July 19, 1966

On the evening of Tuesday, July 19, 1966, three armed men entered the second-floor office of the Rehtstein Flour Co., Rutherford Avenue, Charlestown, bound and gagged the owners, and took more than $40,000. in cash. All three gunmen wore sun glasses and straw hats.

Armored Car Robbery, Bedford, July 22, 1966

Shortly before noon on Friday, July 22, 1966, four masked men, two armed with machine guns, held up a Brink's Armored Truck near the front entrance of the Mitre Corporation in Bedford, where they were about to make a delivery. The gunmen took $131,268. in cash and $16,000. in checks.

Armored Car Robbery, Jamaica Plain, July 26, 1966

About noon on Tuesday, July 26, 1966, three masked men, armed with machine guns, held up an armored car of the Armored Banking Service of Lynn and took $68,000. in cash. Two guards on the truck were shot during the commission of this crime.

Diamond Larceny, Boston, October 6, 1966

About 9:50AM on October 6, 1966, a jewelry salesman, after parking his car, had a green attache case snatched from his hand on Boylston Street, Boston by one man, described as MW, 25-30 yrs., 6', 180-200 lbs., wearing tan trousers and a wind-breaker. The case contained about $75,000. in uncut diamonds.

SOME UNSOLVED BANK ROBBERIES (1966 ONLY)

Worcester Co. Inst. for Savings	4-21-66	WORCESTER	1 Subject
Fall River Trust Co.	5-31-66	FALL RIVER	1 "
Guaranty Bank & Trust Co.	6-30-66	LEICESTER	1 "
Safety Fund National Bank	7-1-66	FITCHBURG	3 Subjects
Market Forge Employees' Credit Union	8-12-66	EVERETT	2 "
First Bank & Trust Co. of Needham	9-16-66	WESTWOOD	2 "
Brookline Savings Bank	10-7-66	BROOKLINE	3 "
First National Bank of Boston	10-10-66	SOUTH BOSTON	2 "

Hacks 'n' Hoods

Essex County Sheriff Charles Reardon, left, another appointee of Gov. Michael Dukakis is sent to prison for taking kickbacks, in 1996.

Joe Barboza taken into protective custody after becoming an informant.

Joe Barboza draws stares in court.

WILLIAM J. HOAR
DOB 10-25-38
ARR 4-14-66 - DIST 6

Warrant DIST 11

attempted murder of
Two Police officers

GET HIM

This "GET HIM" exhortation appears on the back of William Hoar's mugshot.

William Hoar: "foul play suspected"

Indicted high sheriffs Howard Fitzpatrick of Middlesex and Fred Sullivan of Suffolk stand together at Harvard commencement. Both beat raps of "negligence" after high-profile escapes from their jails.

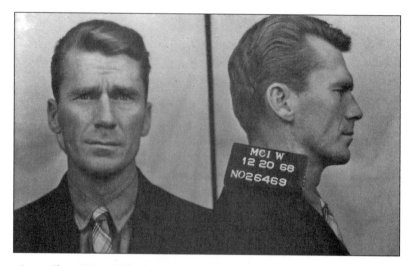

James Flynn: Winter Hill, played the judge in *Good Will Hunting*. He was also an official of Teamsters Local 25, which was then mobbed up.

"Honest" John McGonigle, sheriff of Middlesex County appointed by Gov. Mike Dukakis, taken away in handcuffs by the FBI. After completing his sentence for tax evasion, Honest John was hired by Flynn (above) to work on Local 25's movie crew.

Arthur Gianelli: imprisoned gangster and
brother-in-law of imprisoned FBI agent Zip
Connolly, with actor Jack Nicholson and
Boston Celtic Dennis Johnson.

Convicted felon House speakers Sal DiMasi, Tom Finneran and Charles Flaherty.
On right, House Speaker Bob DeLeo, an unindicted coconspirator in the
probation-department scandal. *Photo courtesy The Lowell Sun.*

Suspect Seized in N. Y. Faces Somerville Quiz

A 25-year-old Charlestown stevedore, arrested by New York police yesterday on violation of the Sullivan (weapons) law, will be questioned by Somerville police in con-

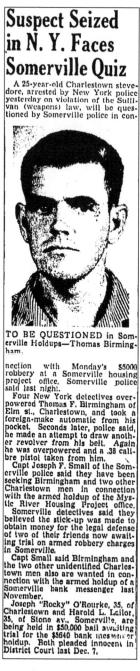

TO BE QUESTIONED in Somerville Holdups—Thomas Birmingham.

nection with Monday's $5000 robbery at a Somerville housing project office, Somerville police said last night.

Four New York detectives overpowered Thomas F. Birmingham of Elm st., Charlestown, and took a foreign-make automatic from his pocket. Seconds later, police said, he made an attempt to draw another revolver from his belt. Again he was overpowered and a .38 calibre pistol taken from him.

Capt Joseph F. Small of the Somerville police said they have been seeking Birmingham and two other Charlestown men in connection with the armed holdup of the Mystic River Housing Project office.

Somerville detectives said they believed the stick-up was made to obtain money for the legal defense of two of their friends now awaiting trial on armed robbery charges in Somerville.

Capt Small said Birmingham and the two other unidentified Charlestown men also are wanted in connection with the armed holdup of a Somerville bank messenger last November.

Joseph "Rocky" O'Rourke, 35, of Charlestown and Harold L. Lailor, 35, of Stone av., Somerville, are being held in $50,000 bail awaiting trial for the $5640 bank messenger holdup. Both pleaded innocent in District Court last Dec. 7.

Chelsea man found murdered

The body of a 42-year-old Chelsea ex-convict was discovered in his blood-splattered bed by police yesterday afternoon after relatives notified them that he had not been seen in several days.

Thomas F. Birmingham of 185 Washington av. suffered head injuries, and police said they believe it to be homicide, but the cause of death was not immediately determined. The result of an autopsy is due today.

A 12-guage shotgun was found on the bed, but police have not identified the owner. It was turned over to ballistics experts.

Birmingham was sentenced to 15-18 years in State Prison in October, 1953, for the armed robbery of the Somerville Housing Authority in February of that year. He had been caught by New York city police, who, on a tip, found him with two loaded revolvers.

He was returned to Somerville and sentenced in Middlesex Superior Court. Two other men took part in the robbery in which six employees of the authority were forced into a vault. Birmingham refused to reveal their names.

He was paroled and arrested again in 1962 on an armed-robbery charge in Providence. He was later sentenced to a 10-year term there and granted parole in 1968.

Thomas Birmingham: uncle of the Senate president
of the same name, murdered 1969

Third from left (with hand over heart), ex-Sen. President Thomas Birmingham, namesake and nephew of slain Charlestown hood Thomas Birmingham. On far right, Whitey Bulger's brother, ex-Sen. president Billy Bulger. To the left of Birmingham in the photo, convicted felon ex-House Speakers Charles Flaherty (income tax evasion) and the balding Thomas "Felon" Finneran (obstruction of justice). Behind Birmingham stands convicted felon ex-House Speaker Sal DiMasi (bribery). The cancer-stricken DiMasi is still serving his sentence in federal prison.

Middlesex County Sheriff James DiPaola facing multiple investigations, committed suicide in Maine, 2012.

Ex-Auditor (and boxer pal of gangsters) Joe DeNucci, with ex-state Treasurer Bob Crane, who used to call Billy Bulger "the little man upstairs."

Alex Rocco, neé Bobo Petricone, as Moe Green in *The Godfather*. "Do you know who I am?"

Bobo returns to Boston in 1973 to film "The Friends of Eddie Coyle."
Kissing him is Howie Winter, to the left is Jimmy Martorano.
At bottom: Robert Mitchum and his driver, Fat Harry Johnson.

Alexander "Bobo" Petricone before he
became the actor "Alex Rocco"

Harry J. Johnson in lighter times

Richie Castucci with Frank Sinatra at Sammy
Davis Jr.'s wedding in Las Vegas

Teddy Deegan's nephew, Gerry Indelicato, was a powerful aide in Gov. Dukakis' corrupt administration. After physically assaulting at least one state rep at the State House, Dukakis made him president of Bridgewater State College, where he was soon indicted for a variety of state and federal crimes, including trying to forge a deed to give himself possession of a parcel of land in the middle of the college campus. Here he is in 1989, listening to sentence being imposed. After serving his state and federal bits, Indelicato became a used-car salesman. His uncle would have been proud.

The Great Plymouth Mail Robbery

For 12 years, the Brinks robbery in the North End was the biggest cash theft in American history—$1.2 million.

But on Aug. 14, 1962, the record fell, both for the United States and Massachusetts, when two bandits pulled over a U.S. mail truck headed north on Route 3 in Plymouth towards the Federal Reserve Bank of Boston. They absconded with $1,551,277 in cash.

It may not have been as complicated as the Brinks job, but the Plymouth heist was intricately planned. The money wasn't in an armored car, it was in a mail truck. Usually, the State Police would have handled delivery of such a large amount of cash, but with the huge summer crowds on the Cape, they were undermanned and begged off.

At around 8 p.m., a car pushed the truck off the road, and a robber dressed as a cop confronted the driver and "guard" with a sawed-off shotgun.

A couple of miles behind the truck, two more men put out signs at the nearest exit to the south, detouring traffic off Route 3. The robbers tied up the two Postal employees, then took off in the truck, making several stops along the way, presumably dropping off a few of the 16 sealed mail pouches in the truck at each location.

The truck was eventually abandoned in Randolph, just off 128, with the two guards still tied up in the back.

It was a huge story, partially because the Post Office had recently been involved in a major public-relations drive, advising Americans not to send cash through the mails due to the increasing number of thefts.

Law enforcement—local, state and federal—pulled out all the stops in trying to crack the case, but to no avail (as you will see). The top suspects included, among others, Carmello Merlino (who would someday be linked to the 1990 Isabella Stewart Gardner Museum heist), Sonny Diaferio, and John "Red" Kelley. The fact that many of the suspects had only the vaguest of connections to one another shows just how "baffled" the cops were.

Finally, in 1967, with the five-year statute of limitations running out, the feds indicted three people—Red Kelley, Sonny Diaferio's blonde wife, and a Weymouth electrician named Thomas Richards. Richards vanished five days before the trial was to begin, was never seen again and was declared legally dead in 1982.

Meanwhile, Kelley and Mrs. Diaferio were acquitted by a jury after less than an hour of deliberations.

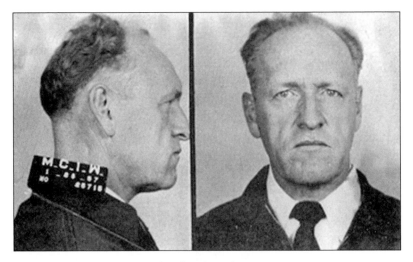

John "Red" Kelley: beat the rap in 1967

Sonny Diaferio

Carmelo Merlino

The money has never been found.

What follows are some reports from a file folder entitled, "Interviews of Top Hoods in Greater Boston Area." They were mainly done by U.S. postal inspectors, operating on the assumption that Merlino and Diaferio were the masterminds.

These interviews provide an instructive snapshot of Boston crime in the 1960's. Most of the hoods wanted to be on record as saying they wouldn't tell the police anything, even if they did know something. (Most apparently didn't.) Of course Whitey Bulger said the same thing. But the fact is, nobody in the Plymouth mail robbery ever snitched—at least not enough to convict anyone.

Two of those interviewed—Teddy Deegan and Joseph Francione— were shot to death by Joe Barboza shortly after their interrogations (for other, non-Plymouth-related reasons). The more interesting sections are highlighted, and material in other interviews lends itself to brief excerpts.

For instance, consider Richard Bellan, also known as "Bucky" or "Moose."

On November 3, 1965, postal inspector F.A. Ricker reported to his control desk:

"In the past three meetings with Bellan, he has asked to borrow money. Although his nickname is 'Moose,' he drinks like a 'fish.' I think that Bellan would like to keep this going for a long time."

Ricker conducted another interview with James E. Marlow, "colored." He had played cards with Sonny and Mello, as Merlino was known.

"Marlow cried 'poor mouth' and indicated that he could not played in a game for anything more than peanuts. He said that he plays 'hearts,' but just for fun.

"He was informed of possible Grand Jury action and stated that he would tell those gentlemen the same as he is telling us: 'If you don't know nothing, you can't tell anybody anything.'"

More significantly, Marlow pointed out he was in jail on Aug. 14, 1962.

Buddy Little, another professional gambler, gave the inspectors a lesson in how not to get cheated when playing with the card sharks who frequented his games:

"Because most of the participants were professionals it was necessary to cut down a box that the cards came in and deal the deck right from the box on the table. In this way no one could mark or bend the cards."

Buddy told the cops he had been running a game since he was 16 years old—"when he first opened the Crib he had a hard time recruiting players and he had an all-colored clientele. Eventually the white boys started to drift in."

Little was shown a mugshot of Kelley but said he didn't recognize him. The postal inspectors mentioned that he was a barbooth player, and Buddy said that explained his unfamiliarity with Kelley.

"Buddy stated that he could not run a (barbooth) game in Boston because he did not have the backing (money) and (his) fear of the hold-up men in the area. He would also have to get permission from 'downtown' before he tried to start."

Billy Cass, interviewed at the Riverway Café on Jan. 16, 1963: "He was given the pitch on the reward for furnishing information and his reply was that he would like to help us out, but he does not know a thing. It is our opinion that if he did, he would not tell us anyway."

Ditto, prisoner Peter Richard Kadra, interviewed on Jan. 17, 1963 at the MCI Forestry Camp in Carver: "Kadra stated that he honestly did not know who was involved in the mail truck robbery but that if he did, it would be against his principles to tell us."

Walter Balben, interviewed at his home in Hudson on Sept. 13, 1962: "Balben lives with his wife, Ruth, and frankly admits or discusses visiting his girlfriend. . . He did state that in his opinion too many cars were used in the robbery. . . Balben stated that if he knew who committed the robbery, he would not inform on them."

The wife of an imprisoned suspect was asked about a friend of hers named Jane: "She states that Jane is not a prostitute, but gives it away to friends."

This woman also mentioned an ex-con named Ralph: "Keeping in mind that Ralph's 'girl friend' when he was in Bridgewater was (redacted), it is possible that Ralph might be a homo. Jean confided that in the 13 months she lived with Carl they were intimate only twice. The second time she got pregnant, but lost the child in a miscarriage."

This was 1965. Today this interview might be described as TMI—too much information.

Gambler, Joe Porro was interviewed at the Thunderbird Hotel in Las Vegas on Dec. 8, 1965, where he "is employed as a barboy." According to another suspect, Joe Tempesta, "Porro has married Tempesta's cousin, Theresa, and had to leave town because shylocks were after him."

Samuel Kalil, Roxbury gambler, interviewed Dec. 8, 1965, a regular at Buddy Little's club, the Crib and Checkers: "He stated that he did not know the true names of the other players. He remembered names such as Nonni, Nunni, Flash, Willie. It was evident that Sam did not care to divulge the true names."

George Christo, convicted robber, interviewed Nov. 6, 1962, was offered a chance to take a lie-detector test: "He was advised that taking the test would save him the embarrassment of having his alibi checked. This (was) predicated on the fact that he is a married man with a 12-year-old daughter and was with other girls on the night of the holdup." (He eventually declined to take the test, explaining that although he could pass this one, if he eventually submitted a second polygraph test about another crime, and failed it, the cops would use the fact that he had once passed a polygraph test against him.)

Christo, interviewed again on May 10, 1963: "He told us that he would not do a job that is 'Federal' and no job that would have a big 'score.' He is satisfied with a little b&e job that would net in the neighborhood of $2,000.00."

What follows are some of the other interviews. A few facts about the "hoodlums" interviewed: Walter Bennett was murdered in April 1967 by Stevie Flemmi. Despite what Tommy Callahan told the postal inspectors, he had in fact not quit the rackets, and was wounded a year or so later in the gang wars. When Callahan did retire from "the life" in the late 1960's (he'd been born in 1905) he sold his machine gun to Stevie Flemmi. While Flemmi was on the lam in Montreal in 1973, he lent Callahan's gun to Johnny Martorano, who used it to kill Al Plummer, an associate of Al Angeli.

Subject: Interview of Joseph Ralph Francione

Francione was interviewed at the Watertown Police Station and his
residente, 103 Edenfield Avenue, Watertwwn, on September 10, 1962
by Inspectors McNabb and Ricker.

He provided the alibi that he was with a girl, Joanne Scali, (DA 1-0190)
on the night of the robbery. He picked her up at 7-7:15 pm. They were
supposed to go out to dinner, but instead drove to Stoncham, purchased
steaks, returned home cooked, ate and watched TV. Franchine returned
home 1-2 am. A girl friend of Joanne's, Jenna, arrived 7:30-8 pm and
stayed until 11:00 pm.

Francione was cooperative and brought us to his home and allowed a
search of his quarters. He drives a 1962 XXXXXl Caddy, having owned
a 61 and 60 before. The present one being purchased a Bell Olds, Revere.
The car he drives now is a gray convertible, white roof.

Francione works for Sun Control, a firm who inthalls glass partitions
and frosted glass. He has contracted various post offices, list attached.
He worked at South Postal for several Christmas periods. Haw not
worked xx for the post office for 10-12 years.

He consented to a lie-detector test and on Tuesday, Sept 11 was given
the test, which he cleared.

J. J. McNabb and F. A. Ricker

Joseph Francione:
murdered January 1965

Inspectors Ricker & McNabb

SUBJECT: Questioning of THOMAS A. CALLAHAN on 9/13/62.

Thomas A. Callahan was questioned at his residence at 62 Arborway, Jamaica Plain, Mass. Callahan at first indicated that he would talk to us on the fron steps of his residence but finally consented to our talking to him in his enclosed front porch.

Callahan was asked to state his whereabouts on August 14, 1962 between the hours of 7:00 p.m. and midnight. He stated that he knew exactly where he was during that time, that he could prove it, but that he was not about to tell us. He gave as his reason that he did not wish to embarass certain respectable friends of his by having us go to them to substantiate his presence during the stated period.

Discussion of the possibility of a lie detector test was ended abruptly by Callahan's asking, "Do you think I'm a nut?".

Callahan stated that we could bring the driver and guard on the mail truck to his house and that he would be perfectly willing for them to look him over.

Callahan was asked if he had any opinions on the mail truck job. He replied that he did but that he was not going to give them to us. However, he then stated that he would give us one opinion, this being that whoever pulled the job was stupid to get involved in kidnapping. He also added that we could check his record and we would not find any instance where he had been involved in stealing anything from Uncle Sam.

Callahan stated that he was from the "old school" and that if he did know anything about the hold-up, he wouldn't tell us even if the reward amounted to a "zillion" dollars.

Callahan insists that he is now legitimite and that we could check his income tax records to verify this. He indicated that he had stopped using his muscles and is now using his mind.

Callahan complained bitterly about the publicity he had received during the investigation of this case. He showed us the newspaper (Boston Traveler) which alleged that a principal suspect was a former body guard for a top underworld czar, and that the suspect was a known killer. Callahan contended that everyone knew who the article was referring to and that this publicity was totally unjustified. He stated that his wife was active in cub scout work (a den mother) and other worthwhile activities that brought her in contact with very respectable people, and that such unfavorable publicity was very embarrassing to her and to him.

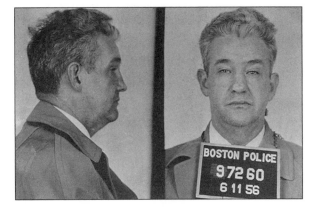

Thomas Callahan: "Do you think I'm a nut?"

Callahan stated that every week-end he and his wife took two children from the Nazareth Home for the entire week-end. He often takes these children, together with his own, to a nearby restaurant for ice cream, etc.

Callahan stated that he did not have a place on the Cape but he appeared to have a good knowledge of the Cape. He remarked that the Cape had improved greatly during recent years, apparently because of the Kennddy influence. He remembers when the super highways, such as the capeway, were only dirt roads. He stated that his nephew is a successful business man in West Yarmouth. (We do not know the identity of the nephew but Callahan told us that the nephew was interviewed by FBI agents on a golf course in the West Yarmouth vicinity, at about the same time he was being interviewed by police and FBI agents at Novicki's place in Dedham in connection with the soil pipe theft).

Callahan is a well spoken person and appears well preserved for his years (57). It was our impression that he was not prone to use profanity except when talking about law enforcement officers. He stated that he had only a grammer school education but that he was well read, a self-educated man. He indicated that his present marriage was his third and that he has three children by his present wife, the youngest being three years of age. He proudly introduced us to his wife, a young and attractive woman.

Callahan stated that he was a sanitation engineer and a carpenter. He was asked where he learned his trades and he replied, "State of Massachusetts". He told us he was doing the carpenter work in Novicki's house, stating that Novicki had helped him previously.

Novicki and Callahan have been described as close associates and this has been substantiated. This association has been particularly evident during recent weeks because of Callahan's helping Novicki with the building of the latter's house. On the date we interviewed Callahan, we also attempted to interview Novicki but we were unsuccessful. We later saw Novicki's car at Callahan's home but we were told by Mrs. Callahan that Mrs. Novicki was visiting her and that Mr. Novicki was not there.

                                                    the
The house under construction is located in/better residential area of Dedham. After completion the house is expected to be in the $40-50,000 bracket. It is the conjecture of police officals that all materials used in the construction have been stolen. The construction site is checked periodically by local pdix police and Callahan is always with Novicki. Recently Lt. Scott of the Dedham Police accompanied Boston City police officers to the construction site. They feel that Novicki saw them coming and took off through the woods in back. A well dressed man was at the site. When questioned he stated that he was a representative of the Perini Construction Firm and was in the process of preparing an estimate. The auto registration was noted and a registration check showed that the xxxxxxx auto was registered to EDWARD CANEJO, Cambridge, Mass., a suspect in this case. Examination of a mug shot on file substaniated the fact that the man visiting Novicki was Canejo.

J.J. McCabb, Jr.
F.R. Kexen

Subject: Interview EDWARD J. McALENEY

McAleney was interviewed at his home, 9 Squirrel Hill Lane, Hingham, Mass., September 18, 1962.

When approached McAleney was very friendly and invited us into his home. He was asked for an alibi for the 14th of August and readily stated that several days before he purchased two filters for his automobiles. The filters did not fit and on Tuesday, the 14th, approximately 8:00 pm he brought them to Jim's Auto Store, Hingham, for exchange. He was accompanied by his wife. A sales slip should be on file at Jim's showing the transaction. McAleney stated that the clerk hit the sales slip and possibly the time could be on the slip.

McAleney is employed at the shipyard at Fore River as a welder. He works daily from 7 am to 3:30 pm.

When asked if he knew Jim Tilley he replied that he was a friend of his and that he heard he had taken a lie detector test on this case. He stated that Jim was dumber than he thought he was. He was then asked if he would be interested in clearing any suspicions by taking the lie box. He replied " Absolutely, Postively Not". He gave as his reason, if he took the box on this robbery, which he knows nothing about and at a later date refuses the test for a crime that he may have knowledge of, it would indicate his implication.

He bluntly refused to discuss the robbery or give his opinion on the job. He refused a seach of his home and auto and said it could only be done if we had " a paper ".

He gave us his unlisted phone number (RI 9 1813) and if we wanted to see him, give him a call and he would arrange, to meet us at any hotel lobby or cocktail lounge. He indicated that he would not visit any government or police office for fear of "bugs" or makeshift lineups.

It was his opinion that any of the suspects would consent to an interview and if contacted by phone would make an appointment. He said it was unwise to bring State Police as nobody would talk, or consent to an interview in their presence.

Johnson-McNabb-Ricker

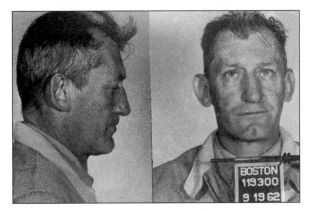

Jim Tilley: "Even dumber than I thought."

January 23, 1963

INTERVIEW ALFRED M # "FREDDIE" SARNO   = S

Freddie Sarno was interviewed at Division Headquarters on
January 18, 1963. He resides at 37 Crescent Ave. Revere, Mass. He
is employed at Sun-Lite Tom. Co. and Ideal Tom. Co. both of which
are owned by his brothers.

Detectives at Station No. 1 advised that they have known
Sarno for a number of years and they consider him to be a big
operator. They did not believe that he would be a participant
in a hold-up but stated that he would be capable to plan a job
of this nature.

Sarno denied knowing any of the principal suspects in this
case. He advised that he had known most of the underworld figures
in Boston a few years ago. He claims that he is now going straight.
Sarno stated that usually after any big job new money appears in
card games and new loan sharks appear. He stated this was true after
the "Brinks" job. Since the Plymouth hold-up he claims there has not
been xxxxxxxxxxxx any new money in circulation and it is his opinion
that whoever pulled this job is sitting on the money. He advised
that money was short and that the limit in most poker games had
been cut from 3 and 6 to 1 and 2.

Sarno was seen talking to Joey Palladino on Sept. 19, 1962,   = S
at North Station. When questioned about this Sarno advised that
Palladino had been attempting to borrow $3,000.00 in order to
get a transcript of his trial and to possibly obtain a new trial.
Sarno stated that if Palladino had been in on the mail job he
would xxxxxxxxxxxxxxxxxxxxxxxxxxxxxxxxxxxxxx have used some of
the money to obtain a new trial rather than go to jail.

Sarno stated that the rewards in this case looked very attractive to him. He claimed that if any new money showed up of if he
obtained any information about the Plymouth hold-up he would contact
us.

J. R. Carroll

F. A. Richu

Sarno denied knowing Agisotelis, Kelly, Richards, or Tripoli

Freddie Sarno claimed he was "going straight."

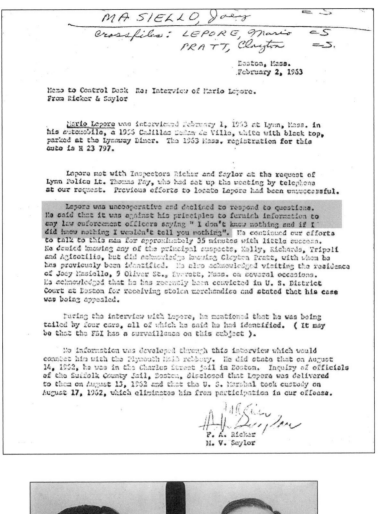

MA SIELLO, Joey
Crossfiles: LEPORE, Mario <S
PRATT, Clayton =S.

Boston, Mass.
February 2, 1953

Memo to Control Desk Re: Interview of Mario Lepore.
From Ricker & Saylor

Mario Lepore was interviewed February 1, 1953 at Lynn, Mass. in his automobile, a 1953 Cadillac Sedan de Ville, white with black top, parked at the Lynnway Diner. The 1953 Mass. registration for this auto is H 23 797.

Lepore met with Inspectors Ricker and Saylor at the request of Lynn Police Lt. Thomas Fay, who had set up the meeting by telephone at our request. Previous efforts to locate Lepore had been unsuccessful.

Lepore was uncooperative and declined to respond to questions. He said that it was against his principles to furnish information to any law enforcement officers saying " I don't know nothing and if I did know nothing I wouldn't tell you nothing". We continued our efforts to talk to this man for approximately 35 minutes with little success. He denied knowing any of the principal suspects, Kelly, Richards, Tripoli and Agisotilio, but did acknowledge knowing Clayton Pratt, with whom he has previously been identified. He also acknowledged visiting the residence of Joey Masiello, 9 Oliver St., Everett, Mass. on several occasions. He acknowledged that he has recently been convicted in U. S. District Court at Boston for receiving stolen merchandise and stated that his case was being appealed.

During the interview with Lepore, he mentioned that he was being tailed by four cars, all of which he said he had identified. (It may be that the FBI has a surveillance on this subject).

No information was developed through this interview which would connect him with the Plymouth Mail robbery. He did state that on August 14, 1962, he was in the Charles Street jail in Boston. Inquiry of officials of the Suffolk County Jail, Boston, disclosed that Lepore was delivered to them on August 13, 1962 and that the U. S. Marshal took custody on August 17, 1962, which eliminates him from participation in our offense.

F. A. Ricker
M. V. Saylor

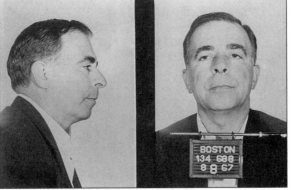

Mario Lepore: later acquitted of murdering Rocco DiSeglio

DEEGAN, Teddy = S

crossfiles: AGISOTELIS Res. #m. = I
HANNON, Harold = S
McLAUGHLIN, Edw. ("Punchy") = S

January 24, 1963

Interview Teddy Deegan relative to his association with Billy Aggie. = S, 1

Inspectors J. R. Carroll and F. A. Ricker

As a result of information received from LF's informant Teddy Deegan was interviewed on this date at his residence, 52 Ashton Street, Everett, Mass.

Deggean was cooperative and invited us into his kitchen. He denied knowing Billy Aggie, Red Kelley, Tommy Richards and Joe Tripoli. He further denied knowing F. Lee Bailey. His only prison confinements were at Deer Island and Dedham County Jail, therefore he could not have made prison buddies with any of the suspects.

He stated that he knew Harold Hannon, Punchy McLaughlin and the rest of the = S, S McLaughlin gang. He could, or would not tell us were Punchy was at the present time.

Degeen would not comment on the mail robbery and offered no suggestions that would be beneficial.

The subject of reward and becoming an informant were discussed with him, however it is our opinion that he was not receptive to either.

Degeen stated that he was employed as a construction worker and indicated that he did mason work. Examination of his hands during the interview disclosed that that were not calloused and his fingernails were well manicured. His hand-shake was weak and his hands smooth. This feature is mentioned in that it is our opinion that Degeen derives his livelihood from other means than working.

A 1959, Gray Lincoln was parked outside his home bearing Mass. Reg 727091 this plate has not been checked out as yet.

Degeen's photo is herewith for filing in the mug book and to show the witnesses in the case in that he fits the general description of " Buster"

rjc—far

1·24-63

Teddy Deegan: cops
checked his hands

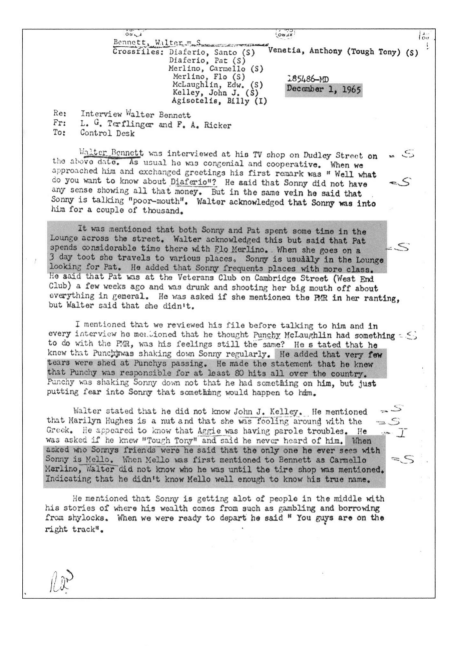

Bennett, Walter M. S.
Crossfiles: Diaferio, Santo (S)   Venetia, Anthony (Tough Tony) (S)
           Diaferio, Pat (S)
           Merlino, Carmello (S)
           Merlino, Flo (S)
           McLaughlin, Edw. (S)   185486-MD
           Kelley, John J. (S)   December 1, 1965
           Agisotelis, Billy (I)

Re: Interview Walter Bennett
Fr: L. G. Terflinger and F. A. Ricker
To: Control Desk

      Walter Bennett was interviewed at his TV shop on Dudley Street on
the above date. As usual he was congenial and cooperative. When we
approached him and exchanged greetings his first remark was " Well what
do you want to know about Diaferio"? He said that Sonny did not have
any sense showing all that money. But in the same vein he said that
Sonny is talking "poor-mouth". Walter acknowledged that Sonny was into
him for a couple of thousand.

      It was mentioned that both Sonny and Pat spent some time in the
Lounge across the street. Walter acknowledged this but said that Pat
spends considerable time there with Flo Merlino. When she goes on a
3 day toot she travels to various places, Sonny is usually in the Lounge
looking for Pat. He added that Sonny frequents places with more class.
He said that Pat was at the Veterans Club on Cambridge Street (West End
Club) a few weeks ago and was drunk and shooting her big mouth off about
everything in general. He was asked if she mentioned the PMR in her ranting,
but Walter said that she didn't.

      I mentioned that we reviewed his file before talking to him and in
every interview he mentioned that he thought Punchy McLaughlin had something
to do with the PMR, was his feelings still the same? He s tated that he
knew that Punchy was shaking down Sonny regularly. He added that very few
tears were shed at Punchys passing. He made the statement that he knew
that Punchy was responsible for at least 80 hits all over the country.
Punchy was shaking Sonny down not that he had something on him, but just
putting fear into Sonny that something would happen to him.

      Walter stated that he did not know John J. Kelley. He mentioned
that Marilyn Hughes is a nut and that she was fooling around with the
Greek. He appeared to know that Aggie was having parole troubles. He
was asked if he knew "Tough Tony" and said he never heard of him. When
asked who Sonnys friends were he said that the only one he ever sees with
Sonny is Mello. When Mello was first mentioned to Bennett as Carmello
Merlino, Walter did not know who he was until the tire shop was mentioned.
Indicating that he didn't know Mello well enough to know his true name.

      He mentioned that Sonny is getting alot of people in the middle with
his stories of where his wealth comes from such as gambling and borrowing
from shylocks. When we were ready to depart he said " You guys are on the
right track".

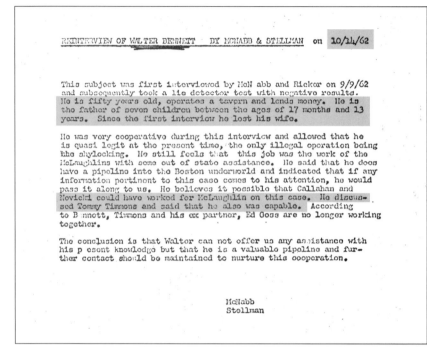

REINTERVIEW OF WALTER BENNETT BY McNABB & STELLMAN on 10/14/62

This subject was first interviewed by McNabb and Ricker on 9/9/62 and subsequently took a lie detector test with negative results. He is fifty years old, operates a tavern and lends money. He is the father of seven children between the ages of 17 months and 13 years. Since the first interview he lost his wife.

He was very cooperative during this interview and allowed that he is quasi legit at the present time, the only illegal operation being the shylocking. He still feels that this job was the work of the McLaughlins with some out of state assistance. He said that he does have a pipeline into the Boston underworld and indicated that if any information pertinent to this case comes to his attention, he would pass it along to us. He believes it possible that Callahan and Novicki could have worked for McLaughlin on this case. He discussed Tommy Timmons and said that he also was capable. According to Bennett, Timmons and his ex partner, Ed Goss are no longer working together.

The conclusion is that Walter can not offer us any assistance with his present knowledge but that he is a valuable pipeline and further contact should be maintained to nurture this cooperation.

McNabb
Stellman

Edward Goss: later became garage attendant at agency controlled by Billy Bulger; convicted of theft and imprisoned

Thomas Timmons: murdered by Mafia 1968

✱ CREAN, Wm. ("Buddy") = S
Crossfiled: AGISOTELIS, Geo. Wm. = S   1-21-63
✱ MASIELLO, Jean (mrs.) = S

Interview William "Buddy" Crean, an associated of Billy A.

F. A. Ricker
J. R. Carroll

Buddy Crean, currently serving 18-25 years in Norfolk for the Marlborough, Mass bank job was scheduled to be interviewed because of his association with Billy Aggie and the report that he was familiar with the operations of Mrs. Jean Masiello, 9 Oliver Street, Everett, Mass, report to be another "Ma Barker".

Norfolk prison was visited and an attempt was made to interview Crean. When he learned our identity he refused to takk to us and stalked out of the room. He stated that he did not want anything to do with " you fu kers" and to go and do a physical impossibility.

The deputy warden stated that since Crean was incarcerated at the time of our robbery, it would be foolish to make him sit through an interview as he has an intense hatred of law inforcement officals. Review of Crean's personnel folder disclosed that all reports indicate his hatred of law enforcement officals.

It is felt that Crean's outburst and refusal was a show put on for the benefit of other convicts working in the area.

✳ Correct spelling
is Crehan, Wm. Joseph   FA Ricker
RJ Carroll

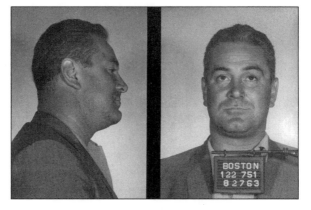

Buddy Crehan: "You fu*kers!"

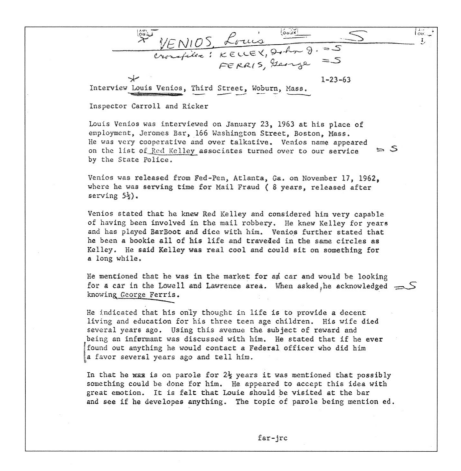

VENIOS, Louis — S

Crossfile: KELLEY, John J. = S
FERRIS, George = S

1-23-63

Interview Louis Venios, Third Street, Woburn, Mass.

Inspector Carroll and Ricker

Louis Venios was interviewed on January 23, 1963 at his place of
employment, Jeromes Bar, 166 Washington Street, Boston, Mass.
He was very cooperative and over talkative. Venios name appeared
on the list of Red Kelley associates turned over to our service ⇒ S
by the State Police.

Venios was released from Fed-Pen, Atlanta, Ga. on November 17, 1962,
where he was serving time for Mail Fraud (8 years, released after
serving 5½).

Venios stated that he knew Red Kelley and considered him very capable
of having been involved in the mail robbery. He knew Kelley for years
and has played BarBoot and dice with him. Venios further stated that
he been a bookie all of his life and traveled in the same circles as
Kelley. He said Kelley was real cool and could sit on something for
a long while.

He mentioned that he was in the market for a car and would be looking
for a car in the Lowell and Lawrence area. When asked, he acknowledged ⇒ S
knowing George Ferris.

He indicated that his only thought in life is to provide a decent
living and education for his three teen age children. His wife died
several years ago. Using this avenue the subject of reward and
being an informant was discussed with him. He stated that if he ever
found out anything he would contact a Federal officer who did him
a favor several years ago and tell him.

In that he is on parole for 2½ years it was mentioned that possibly
something could be done for him. He appeared to accept this idea with
great emotion. It is felt that Louie should be visited at the bar
and see if he developes anything. The topic of parole being mention ed.

far-jrc

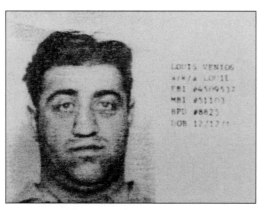

LOUIS VENIOS
A/K/A LOUIE
FBI #4509532
MBI #51103
BPD #8825
DOB 12/12/11

Louis Venios: Combat Zone hood

"The Hill is Us"

It was 3:53 a.m. on April 3, 1981—the morning the Winter Hill Gang merged with the Boston branch of La Cosa Nostra.

More than 32 years later, in the fall of 2013, a minor North End hoodlum named Jerry Matricia would recall the terror he felt that morning, as he was put on the spot by made men of the Mafia over an unpaid debt he owed to Winter Hill.

"I would've said I killed Kennedy that night just to get out of there," he said under oath in the trial of another small-time Mafia gangster, Enrico Ponzo.

Of course the two mobs had been together for almost a decade, since Whitey Bulger had come up with the idea of each gang going after "unaffiliated" bookies, grabbing whoever they could, with the bookie being forced to go with—that is, pay "rent" to—whichever organization grabbed him first.

Since then the two groups had coexisted peacefully. As a favor to "In Town," the Winter Hill Gang had wiped out a renegade faction run by the late Indian Al Angeli, killing six men and wounding several others, including innocent bystanders, in the process. On another occasion, the "In Town" crew had brought over to the Hill's garage on Marshall Street a

Enrico Ponzo in his days as
a young Boston hood

Enrico Ponzo later became
a Montana cattle rancher

The late Al Angeli: in happier times

Larry Baione's headquarters at 51 North Margin Street. Then
the Godfather, now the Dogfather, a doggy day-care center.

visiting LCN delegation from New York seeking money owed one of their
protected bookies. One of the New York Mafioso had even done federal
time with Winter Hill partner Whitey Bulger. But that day the Hill had
stared down the New York crew—much to the delight of underboss Jerry
Angiulo. It reflected well on him in New York, he thought, that he had such
a ruthless crew of cutthroats at his command.

Until this morning, the police had never been able to prove that the two
gangs were now one. But the FBI had bugs planted, not just in Angiulo's
headquarters at the "Dog House" at 98 Prince Street, but at street boss Larry
Baione's headquarters around the corner at 51 North Margin Street, across the
street from Regina's Pizza. In the upstairs apartment, a Mafia soldier named
Johnny Cincotti ran a high-stakes, after-hours card game for a number of
local LCN elder statesmen, including Jerry Angiulo and Larry Baione.

Baione had been raised on Shawmut Avenue in the South End, and later
moved to Jamaica Plain, and finally to Swampscott. So 51 North Margin
Street was where he hung his hat In Town. Late at night, drunk, he liked to
gather his "regime" together and regale them with stories of his love for them.

"I must know what youse are doing," he mused on April 23, 1981. "Jesus
Christ, just give me the respect that I give you people, that's all I want. Then

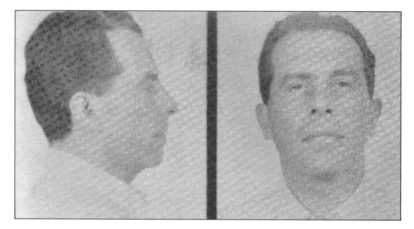

Larry Baione: high school nickname was "Zip."

I'll never let any fuckin' body hurt any fuckin' one of you. . . . 'Cause all of you are basically a beautiful fuckin' guy."

Matricia had never been to 51 North Margin, but this morning he was making a command appearance. His problems dated back to the late 1970's. Martricia had been living in Las Vegas when he got a call from Boston. Winter Hill had set up an elaborate horserace-fixing racket, and was always in need of people to place bets on the rigged races.

Somebody suggested Matricia, and he was given $10,000 by the Hill's top guys, Howie Winter and Johnny Martorano. Matricia put the money on the right horse and won $55,000. A nice score, and his cut would have been at least 10 percent, but as a degenerate gambler, Matricia knew he could do better.

He started betting with the Hill's money, and soon it was all gone, even the original $10,000. Matricia shrugged it off; he was in Vegas, and the gangsters who were furious at him back in Boston. But then Vegas got a little hot—he had stolen a load of marijuana from a car whose owner he claimed not to know.

Soon Matricia had returned to Boston and was running with his old friend Johnny Cincotti. He'd been the bartender at the Nite Lite the night two of Joe Barboza's hoods were clipped there in 1966 and $78,000 in bail money for the Animal was stolen. When the cops arrived the next morning, they found Cincotti trying to clean the blood stains off the floor.

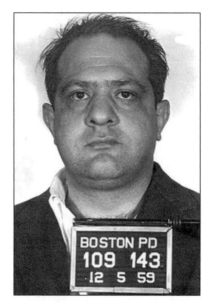

Nicky Giso: In Town soldier

The only Mafioso to take a fall on that double homicide was Ralphie Chong—Ralph Lamattina, another member of Larry Baione's crew.

Baione had a severe drinking problem—after his conviction in 1986, he tried to explain to the judge that most of his incriminating statements were nothing more than drunken rants. Usually his first words upon entering a room were, "Somebody open a bottle of wine."

This morning, Baione had called in Cincotti because he was worried what might happen if the Winter Hill bosses who weren't in prison or on the lam for the race-fixing scheme ever saw Matricia with Cincotti.

Baione was sitting in his office with Ralphie Chong and another of his crew, Nicky Giso. He called in his soldier, Cincotti.

"We got to get something straight here, Johnny. This Jerry, I know you're stealing with him and you're making a living with him. He cut the Hill for like 50,000."

RALPHIE CHONG: "They trusted him with the money."

BAIONE: "Give the kid a chance. Let him talk. He ain't a bad kid."

Ralphie Chong

Ralphie Chong surveillance photo

Matricia was brought in. His partner Johnny Cincotti told him, "Sit down. Shut the door."

Larry Baione would take charge now. His reputation preceded him, as Jerry Matricia would later say. He was suspected of burning bodies at his family's pig farm in Stoughton, and the story was that he had once stabbed a waiter to death for slow service.

Baione was a theoretician of murder, as he proved again and again on the tapes, both at the Doghouse and on North Margin Street.

"If you're clipping people, I always say, make sure you clip the people around him first. He could be the dirtiest motherfucker in the world, but someone that likes this guy, that's the guy that sneaks you."

Baione talked openly about murdering people.

"I want to kill Harvey Cohen very shortly," he told two of his underlings one night. "Have we done anything yet? Shouldn't he be dead by now? This is for the Family in New York. Now I'm responsible."

They had the usual excuses—"that Jew he's always got four or five guys around him." Or "I can't find his house. There's no number, Larry."

Larry Baione doesn't want to hear any more excuses. He quotes the Man, Raymond Patriarca.

"You know what Raymond said? 'Give me a good driver and a machine gun and I'll kill the whole fuckin' mob.' Right? Give me a driver and a machine gun. That's only two guys. Well, I got more than two. . . the Boss and the Underboss give us the work. Why they give us the work? Because they've got the confidence in us. . . So why are you going to louse me up?"

In 1981, Baione was 60 years old, at the height of his underworld power, a stone killer, and he was drunk. Matricia was petrified, as well he should have been. Baione was speaking.

"Jerry, I have to ask you some questions. Sit over here. Jerry. Johnny likes you very much. You understand? I don't know you."

Matricia, scared shitless: "Right."

"I love Johnny very much. So because I love Johnny very much I like you. Same for Ralph, same for Nicky. But one thing we do, Jerry. If you fuck someone that's friendly with us. . . ."

Matricia tried to get up to leave. He had a bad feeling about where this conversation was headed.

"Sit down," Ralphie Chong told him. "Stay awhile. Here."

Larry went back into his lecture, and this was the part that the feds would use more than a decade later to show that "In Town" and Winter Hill were one and the same.

"Now, if you fuck someone that's close to us, I'm going to give you a shake now. So you understand me. Do you know that the Hill is us? Maybe you didn't know that, did you?"

MATRICIA: "No, I didn't."

BAIONE: "Did you know Howie (Winter) and Stevie (Flemmi), they're us. We're the fuckin' Hill with Howie. You didn't know that?"

MATRICIA: "Up to now, I didn't know. I know it now, now that you –"

BAIONE: "Well tell me what you fucked them for."

MATRICIA: "Fifty-one, fifty-one five."

BAIONE: "And you don't want to pay it?"

Now Matricia went into a song-and-dance about how Johnny Martorano, another one of the Hill partners who was then on the lam, had seen him in Vegas and told Matricia that they'd work out a repayment plan later. Larry Baione just kept staring at him.

MATRICIA: "Just tell me who I give it to."

BAIONE: "I know 5000 you made quick. You never gave nothing to nobody, right?"

MATRICIA: "Right. But I didn't know who to give it to."

BAIONE, pointing at Cincotti. "Your man. Right here. Johnny Cincotti. That's who you give it to. And he goes and sees Stevie. Five hundred once in a while."

MATRICIA: "I, I would do that gladly. I would do that gladly. I would do that gladly. I've still got, there's a balance left with them."

BAIONE, chuckling: "Oh, I know there's a balance."

Now Baione tries to explain to Matricia that the money, paltry as it may seem, means a lot to the Hill. This was a couple of years before they got into drugs, bigtime, collecting a million dollars per boatload of marijuana shipped into the Harbor, and dealing their own cocaine in Southie. At this point, they owed Jerry Angiulo $245,000 they'd borrowed to prop up their now-failed bookmaking racket—"their own fuckin' headache," as Baione described it.

"These kids haven't got 30 cents, between you and me, to start off with. These are not big money guys. They owe their fuckin' life. Did you know that? You probably didn't know that?"

"No," says Matricia, yet again, "I didn't know that."

Again, Matricia brought up the name of Johnny Martorano, who was, conveniently enough, hiding out in Florida and thus unavailable to contradict anything that Matricia was saying.

"Johnny told me," Matricia said, "he says, 'Anybody asks you, you tell them you're even with me, and Shorty McDuff and Mel Golden.'"

If Matricia had thought he might impress Baione by dropping those names, he didn't succeed.

"Shorty McDuff?" Baione sneered. "Don't mention Mel Golden. Don't mention Golden or Shorty. They're two assholes. Shorty McDuff is the biggest fuckin'. . . a weasel of a cocksucker."

On that note, Matricia was sent back outside Baione's inner sanctum, while he, Ralphie Chong and Cincotti discussed the situation. Ralphie Chong recalled telling Cincotti, "Johnny, I don't want you to be with that kid when you go over there (to East Boston) because this kid is going to get clipped.' Do you remember that?"

Cincotti remembered that.

Ralphie Chong: "They were going to hit this kid. I know if Stevie or Whitey sees him –"

"—they're going to hit him," Baione said. "Yes, they are."

"I know I would," said Ralphie Chong. "Wouldn't you?"

"What I'm trying to do is prevent that." Larry Baione, peacemaker.

Ralphie Chong explains how he wanted to discuss this outside of Matricia's presence.

"Well, fuck him!" Baione snarls.

RALPHIE CHONG: "Did you know that they're still hot at him?"

BAIONE: "Of course I know. What the fuck do you think I'm telling him he's got to pay some fuckin' money here. If they weren't hot at him, I'd say, fuck it kid. Wait 'til they get mad at you."

Nicky Giso, who had been listening silently, finally piped up with another suggestion. Nicky's solution was always to hit somebody. He once tried to set up his girlfriend to be murdered. He told her to wear a cowboy hat she'd just bought down to the Nite Lite because it turned him on. After she got there, two guys in masks walked in and started shooting at her.

"If you want to clip someone tell him, tell everybody you paid it (the debt to Winter Hill)."

"Yeah," said Baione, "and then crack him."

"We won't get the blame," Giso explained. In other words, since we'd settled up with him, why would we kill him?

New England Mafia boss Raymond L.S.
Patriarca didn't like reporters

In 1938, Patriarca bribed a Governor's
Councilor in Massachusetts to
get a commutation.

By now, Matricia was back in the room. Whether he heard Giso's alternate plan for him is lost to history, but Baione began by trying to lull him.

"Jerry," he said, "you know, we've got all the respect in the world for you. I don't know you. But Johnny is a nice man, and everybody in this fuckin' country respects Johnny. And you're with Johnny and you're with the best guy. You couldn't be with any better guy. Just put that in your fuckin' head."

That was the carrot. Now came the stick.

"But Johnny will not tolerate you fuckin' people because you're with him. I know you're out in a fuckin' scuffle. But you better curtail. And whatever you do, you tell Johnny. Do you understand?"

At this point the FBI transcript of the conversation changes. Instead of replies, the only response from Matricia is recorded as ". . . ." Because he had no response, he was so frightened.

"You make sure," Baione said, "you make a score, you pay. I'm going to see Whitey and Stevie get the money, and Howie. You understand? After all you fucked them, didn't you?"

Matricia: . . . .

"You out and out fucked them."

Matricia: . . . .

"But you don't fuck them because they're with us. Are they with us? Are they with us?"

"A thousand percent." This is John Cincotti speaking now.

"These are nice people," Larry says of his crew of Winter Hill hitmen. "These are the kind of fuckin' people that straighten a thing out. They're with us. We're together. And we cannot tolerate them getting fucked. Okay?"

Matricia finally has to respond. "Okay Larry." Then he says that he will "gladly" give Johnny 75 percent of whatever he makes, just to get out of this hole he's in. "Gladly," like Wimpy in the Popeye cartoons, gladly paying Tuesday for a hamburger today.

"Good enough," Larry says, relaxing. "Good enough."

"Is that okay?" Matricia asks, pleads.

"Johnny likes you," Baione says. "Johnny convinced me that you're a nice boy and I like you too. What you just said convinced me. That's enough. Okay?"

"Thank you, Larry."

"All right buddy. Thank you."

Jerry Matricia survived. Like so many others he became addicted to co-caine. In the fall of 2013 he was a prosecution witness in federal court, against a mobster who was 12 years old that night in 1981.

Matricia recounted his habit, how he would cut two lines at once—"one for the one nose, one for the other nose," as he put it, apparently mean-ing nostril. He recalled once stealing four ounces of cocaine from a dealer named Goldman, and then snorting it all by himself.

"That's a lot of coke," the mobster's lawyer commented.

"Some people think it is," Matricia said with a shrug. "Some people think it ain't."

Finally the cross-examination got around to the morning of April 3, 1981, when the feds were finally able to prove that the Mafia and the Winter Hill Gang had merged. Matricia still remembered it as if it had happened yesterday.

"I'm talking to a guy who looks like he's gonna kill me in two minutes," he said. "I just agreed to whatever he said."

The lawyer asked him, "Are you afraid of your own words?"

"No," Matricia answered. "But I am afraid of Larry Zannino. His repu-tation precedes him. I was a-scared for my safety that night."

AS FOR Larry Zannino, he was arrested along with the Angiulos in 1983, but after claiming that he had a heart condition, he was tried separately in 1986. Each morning, an ambulance would bring him to court, and he would lie on a cot in the courtroom, moaning occasionally.

After the jury convicted him, he propped himself up on his cot and told them all to go fuck themselves.

In federal prison, he claimed his health was continuing to deteriorate. His son Joey sent a letter to the federal judge who had sentenced him, beg-ging for mercy:

"My father is no angel but he'll soon be with them if you don't release him."

On Feb. 27, 1996, in the federal prison hospital in Springfield, Mo., Larry Baione joined the angels. He was 76 years old.

12

Jewish Gangsters

"Is there any tough Jews around, you motherfucker?"

That was the question Ralphie Chong posed one evening at the Dog-house one evening in April 1981. They were talking, drinking, and the

Ralphie Chong: no friend of Jews

subject turned to a loanshark, apparently Jewish, who was not a favorite of Larry's.

"You probably know why I slapped Charlie Kellum in the face?" Baione asks Jerry Angiulo.

Kellum had a falling out with the Mafia. Baione told him to stop coming around. Jerry was concerned about the ramifications.

"In my opinion Charlie Kellum will go to the feds. He is –"

"Let him go to the feds and fuck himself," Larry Baione says. "What he did to me, he deserved to get his balls –"

"You think you could be wrong?"

"No, no. I know I'm right. I want to put it on record so you won't say Jesus, Larry, did you slap Kellum in the mouth?"

Apparently Larry had thrown Kellum out of a card game, on general principles. Kellum wanted back in. So one afternoon, when Larry was sunning himself on the back deck of his home in Swampscott, Kellum showed unannounced. Now he has Jerry's full attention. No more defense of Kellum. The underboss is appalled at this breach of etiquette, not to mention security.

Phil Waggenheim:
"Hole in the head"

ANGIULO: "Dirty fuckin' rotten Jew cocksucker."

BAIONE: "(I said) 'Get out. Get out you.'"

ANGIULO: "You can't give them a fuckin' inch, you know that."

Which was when Ralphie Chong posed his question.

BUT THE fact is, yes there were some tough Jews in Boston throughout most of the 20th century.

Phil Waggenheim was usually described as a "hitman" for In Town, as the local Mafia was called. As you

George Kaufman: from
Wimpy to Winter Hill

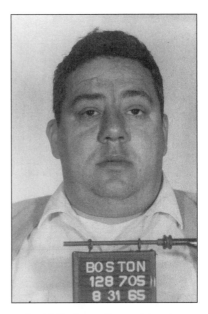

David Kaufman: George's brother

might expect, the nickname came from an early attempt on his life that he survived. Waggenheim got along well with Whitey Bulger, and sometimes hung out at his garage in the West End.

Kaufman spent his life in the rackets. He started out working for Wimpy Bennett, the famous Roxbury gangster. After Stevie Flemmi murdered his boss and buried him in Hopkinton, Kaufman sold Bennett's Cadillac for $6,000.

Later, Kaufman served as the liaison between fugitive hitman Johnny Martorano and his conniving partners, Bulger and Flemmi. By the time the gang was indicted in 1995, Kaufman was dying of cancer. Flemmi sent out the word to everyone: when the feds call you in, blame everything on Kaufman. It doesn't matter to him.

It didn't. He died in 1996. Kevin Weeks and another gang member were sent to his home in Brookline, where the gang had stored an arsenal in the attic. Working in the dark, they overlooked one machine gun. Imagine the surprise of the home's new owner when he went up to survey his attic and found an AR-15.

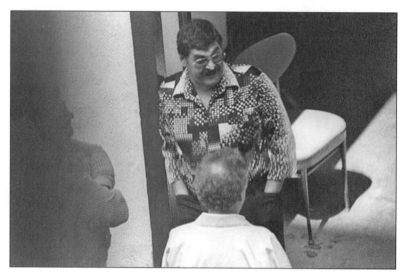

Kaufman with bookie Charlie Raso

Kaufman and Whitey Bulger

Bookie Mel Berger gets some fresh air outside George Kaufman's garage

Howie Levinson, bookie, with George Kaufman outside Kaufman's West End garage, which served as Whitey Bulger's headquarters in the early 1980s

KING SOLOMON flourished during Prohibition. He was the biggest Jewish gangster in New England, working with Dan Carroll of South Boston, smuggling bootlegged booze into New England. He did a short federal bit for obstruction of justice—he paid a witness to lie in a narcotics trial in which he was found not guilty. Serving time in Atlanta, Rep. James Gallivan (for whom Gallivan Boulevard is named) wrote a letter urging his return to a prison closer to New England.

In 1927, he attended the famous Atlantic City Conference of mobsters sponsored by Nucky Johnson of later *Boardwalk Empire* fame.

Charles "King" Solomon: Prohibition rumrunner

King Solomon was shot to death in the men's room of the Cotton Club in January 1933 by two small-time Irish mobsters, who were later acquitted of the murder. Solomon was 49.

Lou Fox (right): North Shore "sportsman"

LOU FOX was one of Solomon's deputies, who inherited the incredibly corrupt city of Revere just north of Boston. "LF" ruled Revere until he suffered a fatal heart attack while driving in 1963. In his obituaries he was described as a "North Shore sportsman."

Maurice "Marsy" Lynch, Fox's underboss, tried to keep LF's organization intact, but the Mafia quickly moved in to the fill the void in what was then a predominantly Italian-American community.

Maurice lynch: Fox's underboss

HARRY "DOC JASPER" SAGANSKY was one of Boston's most connected underworld figures, even though he had no gunmen. He was a major figure in gambling circles. Every so often, usually just before elections, police would raid his gambling joints, and pictures such as the one below of this lineup would appear in the newspapers.

A trained dentist, Doc became incredibly wealthy. During one police raid in Charlestown in 1943, cops discovered a life-insurance policy on once-and-future mayor James Michael Curley. Between political offices, Curley had apparently gone to Doc Jasper for a loan, and for collateral, Sagansky had insisted on being named as the beneficiary of a life-insurance policy.

In those days, Doc Jasper owned nightclubs as well as three racetracks.

Harry "Doc Jasper" sagansky:
Tufts-trained dentist

The lineup in 1943: Doc is second from left

According to reports, he employed as many as 3000 people. After his organized-crime hearings in 1950, Tennessee Sen. Estes Kefauver concluded that Sagansky in the early 1940's was "perhaps the principal gambling racketeer" in New England.

After the fall of the Angiulos in the 1980's, Doc Jasper, now in his late 80's, was brought in by the new Mafia bosses to their bakery in the Prudential Center, which the FBI had bugged. He was accompanied by Moe Weinstein, his associate, who was in his 70s.

The new, younger, dumber hoods told Sagansky he was going to have to pay more for "protection." He pointed out to them that his numbers business had basically been destroyed by the Mass. State Lottery, and offered to turn everything over to the Mafia, free of charge.

No, they said, we want $75,000, and we're keeping Moe until you come up with the dough. The Mafioso then

Moe Weinstein: Doc Sagansky lieutenant

put Doc and Moe in a back room, also bugged by the FBI, where they could decide what to do. Doc Sagansky asked Moe what he thought.

"I guess you're going to have to pay it," Moe Weinstein said.

The next morning, Sagansky delivered a bag with $75,000 cash to the Parker House. Later, he was called before a federal grand jury, but refused to reveal what had happened. At the age of 90, he was slapped with an 18-month sentence for contempt, which he served, and then returned to Boston. He died in 1998 at the age of 101.

Wady David: drug "kingpin"

WADY DAVID was a South End-based criminal who was shot to death by parties unknown in 1965 (See "The Departed.")

Ed Swartz ran a bookie operation out of his Mass. Ave. business. In the early 1960's, a TV network put hidden cameras across the street to record a parade of people, including uniformed cops, going in and out of his business. After the national uproar died down, Swartz took a pinch, served a few months and then returned to business at the same old stand.

Ed Fishbein briefly employed Joe Barboza as a collector/legbreaker. This allowed Barboza at one point to identify his business as "International Public Relations" for Fishbein.

Most of the Jewish criminals were bookmakers. They don't look violent, because they weren't.

Ed Swartz: TV star of sorts

Ed Fishbein: loanshark

Bernard Popkin

Hyman Popkin

Louis Popkin

In the early 1980's, some of them were photographed stopping by the West End garage run by George Kaufman to make their monthly payoffs to Bulger and Flemmi.

Myer Sherman

MEANWHILE, BACK at the Doghouse, Larry Baione was explaining how he let Charlie Kellum back in the game, but then got angry at him, accusing him of screwing him on a loanshark deal that Kellum had.

"Fuckin' Jew. . . fuckin' asshole. . . Bang, I hit him an open-hander."

When Kellum said, "Jesus Christ, Larry, I'm sor-," Baione continued,

"Shut up, you fuckin' Jew cock. . . I said, 'You, you fuckin' Jew, (get the) fuck outta here.' . . . Now this Jew is sayin' 'I'm sorry Larry. I'm sorry.' And I don't even want to listen to him."

Later on, Baione wondered aloud why Charlie Kellum hadn't tried to defend himself.

"What kind of man is he? Take a smack in the mouth and not even move. I wonder. Why didn't he move the other night?"

Perhaps he was frightened. It wasn't really an ethnic thing, this fear of Larry Baione. As Jerry Matricia said of the night he visited Baione, he would have confessed to killing JFK just to get out of 51 North Margin Street alive.

Jimmy "the Bear's" Kodachromes

Of all the serial killers in the Boston underworld in those days, Vincent "Jimmy the Bear" Flemmi may have been the most fearsome. In his confession, Stevie Flemmi said that when the brothers were young, he would always bring a gun to the dinner table, because he was never sure if, or when, "the Bear" would pull out a gun and shoot him.

During his early stretches in prison, "the Bear" developed a severe drug problem, compounded by alcoholism. This made him extremely unstable, and he killed so many people that finally "the Man," Raymond L.S. Patriarca, had to call him down to Federal Hill to inform him that he couldn't settle every argument by shooting whoever he had a dispute with.

Yet he usually did.

Jimmy Flemmi: a "bad boy"

Stevie Flemmi: Jimmy's older brother

Leo Lowry: "the Bear" murdered
"Iggy" in 1964

George Ashe: murdered in 1965, just
after becoming an FBI informant
(which "the Bear" didn't know)

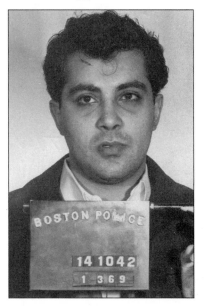

James Abboud: survived
a 1970 stabbing

Jimmy "the Bear" had a family. What follows are some photos from his scrapbook. Of course, given his life of crime, many of the photos of "the Bear" were taken at various state prisons, usually Norfolk, occasionally Walpole.

Jimmy in prison

Always the life—or death—of the party

Brother Stevie makes a rare
appearance in a tuxedo

Pretend it's a mugshot, Bear!

Jimmy holding his baby Tina

Somewhere in the background, a radio was playing "Beach Blanket Bingo."

Merry Christmas from the Jug

Stevie, who would later murder two of his
girlfriends, listens intently to the priest's homily
about the sanctity of the marital vows.

Wearing a hat—Jimmy must be out again—

—but not for long.

"Vote for Dukakis—he'll make sure I get a weekend furlough!"

Visiting day again at MCI–Norfolk

"Whew! Raking the yard is harder than killing some rat!"

As time went on, Jimmy's behavior grew more and more bizarre, and his stints outside prison shorter and shorter.

In 1975, he was granted a weekend furlough by the administration of Gov. Michael S. Dukakis. "The Bear" headed directly for his home in Hyde Park, looking to kill his estranged wife. She heard he was out, and fled immediately.

When "the Bear" arrived at his house, he had to settle for wrecking everything inside. Then he killed his wife's cat. Finally, he fled to Maryland, ironically, just like the more famous beneficiary of the Dukakis weekend-furlough policy, Willie Horton.

(Horton, who had murdered a service-station attendant, got a weekend furlough and bought a winning Lottery ticket. The next time he got out, he cashed in his ticket and used the

Jimmy "the Bear" Flemmi

Jimmy "the Bear" final mugshot;
three months later he would die
of a drug overdose.

Jimmy "the Bear" in a paddy
wagon for the ride "home"

In prison, Jimmy Flemmi
models a new toupee.

Jimmy "the Bear" Flemmi in custody

money to flee to Maryland, where he assaulted and abused a couple. It became a presidential campaign issue in 1988 when the couple came to Boston looking for an apology, and Dukakis refused to meet with them. The issue was first raised in the New York primary by then-Sen. Al Gore, but used much more effectively later by Vice President George H.W. Bush.)

Flemmi was recaptured after beating a woman in Baltimore in 1979, and returned to his second home, MCI-Norfolk. By now his drug problem was out of control. He died of a drug overdose in September 1979.

"What, me worry?"

After he died, his mother Mary went into hysterics at "the Bear" wake. She began screaming, wailing, yelling about her poor son. Finally Stevie had to grab her by the arm.

"Ma," Stevie hissed. "Calm down. He murdered half of Boston!"

Elizabeth Frances Dixon
1948–1968

Many people who died in Boston's gang wars of the 20th century could accurately be described as "innocent victims."

One such person was Liz Dixon. She was from Roxbury, a 1967 graduate of St. Joseph's, a Catholic high school for girls in Roxbury that the Archdiocese has since closed.

She was unemployed, smoked Kools, and had taken up with Hubert "Smitty" Smith, age 47, a man more than old enough to be her father. He was a bouncer at the Basin Street South, a mob-controlled nightspot owned off and on again through the 1960's either by the Martoranos or the Lamattinas.

In 1968 it was run by the Lamattinas, but when Stevie Flemmi got a beating there one night in January, he called Johnny Martorano. He was particularly incensed by what "the nigger" had done to him. What he didn't tell Johnny was that Smitty had just been following orders, from Rocco Lamattina and John Cincotti, two Mob soldiers. Flemmi had been shylocking to one of the younger Lamattinas—one shylock wasn't supposed to do that to another loanshark's family members.

Flemmi had come down to the club on the Roxbury-South End line unannounced and began crowding the kid—all over $300.

The Mafioso told Smitty to pin Stevie's arms back, and the other two did a real number on him.

This is how "Informant" Stevie spun it to H. Paul Rico in his next FBI report:

> Informant stated that recently STEVIE FLEMMI
> had been beaten up by the son-in-law of CARIOCA (uncle to
> RALPH "CHONG" LAMATTINA) over $300 which had been loaned
> to CARIOCA's son-in-law by FLEMMI. Informant stated that
> FLEMMI had tried to collect this from CARIOCA's son-in-law
> and met some fast talk. Informant stated that FLEMMI later
> went back to a bar where CARIOCA's son-in-law was and was
> beaten up by a Negro bartender, CARIOCA's son-in-law and one
> of his friends.
>
> Informant stated that STEVIE FLEMMI was in pretty
> bad shape; however, stated that he would take care of the
> matter himself. Informant stated that he heard that LARRY
> BAIONE indicated that anything STEVIE FLEMMI wanted to do about
> it was alright with him since CARIOCA's son-in-law was wrong
> in doing what he did.

But Stevie called Johnny and put everything on Smitty. That Friday night in January 1968, Johnny went to the club and confronted Smitty. Smitty just shrugged and said that Flemmi had been "way out of line." He didn't explain it wasn't his beef. Enraged, Martorano decided to kill Smitty. He told Smitty he wanted to check out a new after-hours game in Roxbury, but didn't know how to get there, and could he meet Smitty at 3 a.m. on Normandy Street.

Sure, Smitty said.

That morning, in a blinding snowstorm, Flemmi walked up to Smitty's Mercury, saw three shadows, got into the car, pulled out his gun and started shooting. Smitty was killed, as was a 17-year-old boy named Douglas Barrett, who had a quarter and a pack of Tip Top rolling papers in his pocket.

The third victim was Liz Dixon, like the others shot in the head. Her body was in the front seat, next to Smitty's. When the police arrived, she still had a lit Kool between her fingers.

The papers described her as a "go-go dancer." The triple homicide didn't get much play, though. In the Hearst-owned *Sunday Advertiser*, the story ran under a one-column headline on page 47.

What follows are some photos of Elizabeth Dixon from her 1966 high school yearbook.

Basketball

After The Ball

Liz

Page 40

A high-school yearbook photo of Elizabeth Dickson of Roxbury (third from the left), murdered by mistake by John Martorano in 1968, when she was 19

Drill Team

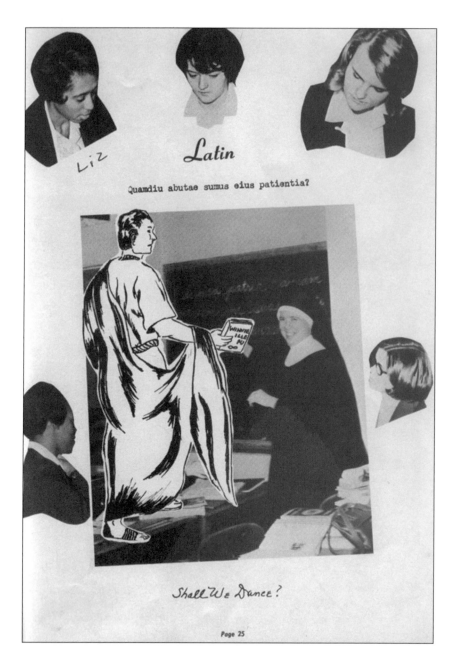

Liz

Latin

Quamdiu abutae sumus eius patientia?

Shall We Dance?

Page 25

Johnny Martorano: Liz Dixon's murderer.
Now 74 years old and living in Milford.

During their desultory murder investigation, the Boston police interviewed Dixon's neighbors. One woman said she'd asked Liz if she really
thought it was a good idea to hang out at a place like Basin Street South.

"Mother said I will be all right," she replied.